Shocking Secrets of Adult Design

Uncensored Marketing Strategies for Starting a Profitable Adult Design Business

Sean Earley

Income Disclaimer:

This document contains business strategies, marketing methods and other business advice that, regardless of my own results and experience, may not produce the same results (or any results) for you. I make absolutely no guarantee, expressed or implied, that by using this document, related software or following the advice below, you will make any money or improve current profits, as there are several factors and variables that come into play regarding any given business. Primarily, results will depend on the nature of the product or business model, the conditions of the marketplace, the experience of the individual, and situations and elements that are beyond your control. As with any business endeavor, you assume all risk related to investment and money based on your own discretion and at your own potential expense.

Liability Disclaimer:

By reading this document, you assume all risks associated with using the advice given below, with a full understanding that you, solely, are responsible for anything that may occur as a result of putting tais information into action in any way, and regardless of your interpretation of the advice.

You further agree that my company cannot be held responsible in any way for the success or failure of your business as a result of the information presented below. It is your responsibility to conduct your own due diligence regarding the safe and successful operation of your business if you intend to apply any of our information in any way to your business operations.

Terms of Use:

You are given a non-transferable, "personal use" license to this product. You cannot distribute it or share it with other individuals. Also, there are no resale rights or private label rights granted when purchasing this document. In other words, it is for your own personal use only. Be nice and don't be a scamming, stealing, shit-eating weasel.

Copyright 2012 by Sean Earley
All Rights Reserved

ISBN-10: 1478290714
ISBN-13: 978-1478290711

Shocking Secrets of Adult Design

Uncensored Marketing Strategies for Starting a Profitable Adult Design Business

Sean Earley

For more great marketing related products, check out:

www.devilishmedia.com

& Join the Mailing List!

Table of Contents

Introduction 11

Chapter One 17
How I Got Started In Adult Design

- The Whole SHOCKING STORY of my journey into the twisted world of adult design.

- Where I started, where I almost crashed and burned, and how I created a successful and profitable business out of the ashes.

Chapter Two 29
The Benefits of Doing Adult Design

- 9 Strategic Reasons why adult design can be a very lucrative business venture with tons of potential.

Chapter Three 33
So... Do You Really Want to Be an Adult Designer?

- Some very important questions to ask yourself BEFORE you get started

- How to decide if "Doing Adult" is right for you.

Chapter Four 37
Uncensored Business & Marketing Strategies

- 5 Strategies that have been the keys to my success as an adult designer.

- A look behind the curtain at my Top Secret Untapped Adult Niche.

- How to create a steady stream of income even when you aren't working.

Chapter Five 59
A Typical Day Designing Porn

- A day in the life, how it REALLY goes down. You think you know, but you have no idea!

Chapter Six 65
Getting to Know The Adult Industry

- How to get started the right way by learning the basics of where the Adult Industry is at in 2012 and what it means for YOU as a designer.

Chapter Seven 73
Know The Law

- How to identify and avoid some very common, and sometimes very costly legal mistakes most people make when getting started in adult.

Chapter Eight 83
Niches and Fetishes

- The secrets of niches and fetishes and how they can help you dominate the competition.

- How to discover untapped profitable adult niche goldmines

Chapter Nine 95
The Portfolio

- The right way to build your portfolio for Maximum Impact and with the LEAST amount of effort.

Chapter Ten 109
Pricing and Billing

- The secrets to pricing, billing and time management.

Chapter Eleven 117
Open for Business

- My Fast and Easy Method for getting your first adult design clients

- How to use social media to tap into an endless flow of adult industry clients

Chapter Twelve 129
Marketing Tips and Tricks

- Some unconventional super secret tactics for promoting your adult design business

Summary 135

Resources 137

Shocking Secrets of Adult Design

WARNING!
✓ Please Read: ✓

This book discusses mature topics and uses language that you may find:

Offensive
Distasteful,
Funny,
Interesting,
Mind Blowing
Witty,
Financially Beneficial,
Disturbing,
Arousing,
Totally Rad
or Just Plain Icky

Consider Yourself Warned

Shocking Secrets of Adult Design

Introduction

Now let me take a wild guess...

You are most likely reading this book right now because at some point in time, the following thought popped into your head:

"You know what? Screw it, I should just do porn..."

That's pretty much how I got started. It was just one of those "Sure, what the hell..." kind of decisions that resulted in the launch of my own adult design business, Devilish Media, over 12 years ago.

What started off as a desperate need to find new clients and pay the bills, quickly evolved into a successful & profitable design, consulting and publishing business, a full time job (whenever I want or need it) and even a way to draw income when I am NOT working.

I now charge a premium rate, I rarely accept new clients and I am very selective when I do. I can pick and choose when I work, where I work, what projects I want to take, and what projects I DON'T want to take.

As a result, I now have a huge client list of famous porn stars, producers, managers, promoters, publicists, hi priced escorts, dominatrixes, rock stars, movie stars, models, best selling authors, corporate executives and even politicians, all who beg me to do work for them.

I know... it's a tough life...

Obviously, now you are thinking:

"Sounds SWEET! So, how do I get in on some of this porn action?"

Well, here's your chance!

Maybe you are just starting out as a designer and doing adult design is your true passion (no pun intended)?

Maybe you have been a designer for quite some time and are just looking for some new clients, new experiences and new revenue streams?

Maybe you have already been approached by some clients to do adult design and are considering if "doing adult" is the right decision for you?

Maybe you're just a curious entrepreneur and looking to pick up some new, top secret, ninja marketing skills and some insanely crazy new niche ideas?

Regardless, this book was written to help you answer many of your burning questions, by giving you an insider's look at how I run a successful and profitable adult design business.

Here's the Golden Ticket

If you've ever read the book "Charlie and the Chocolate Factory" you can think of the rest of this book like this:

I'm Willie Wonka, you're Charlie & what you will learn in this book is the glass elevator and key to my chocolate factory, which I am now passing on to you. The only difference is, instead of chocolate, this factory is full of **Hot Naked Chicks and PORN!** Aw yeah, baby!

What this book is about:

This book is about 12 years of adult design business and marketing secrets and strategies, wrapped up and served up to you on a silver platter. It is also a trip down the rabbit hole into the bizarre and crazy world of adult design.

I'll let you look over my shoulder as I offer up personal insights into adult design, the adult biz, how I got started and how I grew my business into what it is today.

I will be presenting you with some new and unique perspectives, a wealth of new ideas and opportunities for new clients and income possibilities, (as well as advice that can and will save your ass.)

Basically, a big ol' deep dive into the world of adult design.

I will provide you with the most up to date, actionable information as possible, based on my personal experience, in order to make an informed, solid entry into the industry, as well as enough tips and tricks to give you a strategic advantage over your competition.

(Oh, and did I mention, there's porn? Well, at least I talk about it...)

Here's what I'll be covering:

- How I got started as an adult designer.

- Some very important questions to ask yourself BEFORE you get started.

- The benefits of running an Adult Design Business

- My top secret strategies for dominating the competition and building a successful adult design business.

- What a typical day as an adult designer is all about.

- How to get started the right way, by learning the basics of the Adult industry in 2012.

- How to identify and avoid some very common, and often times, very costly legal mistakes that most people make when getting started in the business.

- The real secrets of fetishes and niches and how it can help you dominate the competition.

- The right way to build your portfolio.

- My fast and easy method for getting your first Adult design clients.

- How I use social media to tap into a limitless flow of major adult industry clients and how to keep them once you get them.

- The secrets of pricing, billing & time management.

- How to develop a system to create a steady stream of income even when you aren't working.

- My unconventional, super secret tactics to help you carve out your own unique and profitable niches within the adult industry

What this book is NOT about:

This is NOT a "how to be a designer" book. I am writing this under the assumption that you already have at least a rudimentary understanding of how to design, code and create digital media. (e.g. building websites, blogs, HTML, PHP, Photoshop, apps, etc.)

This is also NOT a generic "how to start a business" book, (i.e. the basics like getting a business license, hiring an accountant or paying your taxes.) There are tons of great books about these two subjects, so if you want something along those lines, go buy a Dummies book on "How to Start a Business in My Area" or "How to Photoshop Boobies" or whatever. I think you get the idea.

However, if you are already a designer and want to learn how to transition your business into the adult industry, then read on, because this is the perfect resource for you.

Suggestion - Read the Entire Book FIRST!

I highly suggest that you read the whole book from front to back BEFORE you get started. It will save you a LOT of time and frustration later. Pay very special attention to the chapter: **Know The Law**. It can and will save your ass some day.

So, with that said, let's jump down the rabbit hole and get started.

Shocking Secrets of Adult Design

Chapter 1

How I Got Started In Adult Design

"Nothing Risqué, Nothing Gained"
– Alexander Woollcott

People do the craziest shit for money... in my case it was starting an adult design business with a clientele of dominatrixes, phone sex operators, and porn stars.

It was never my lifelong dream of starting an adult design business, and was definitely never on my radar as a possible career choice, much less a job description that I can slap on the old resume.

It just kind of, well... happened.

When I started, I was just another unemployed, broke musician, coming off of a tour and desperately needing a new career choice that would pay the bills. I never graduated college and never took any formal graphics courses.

Fortunately, I was always good at art, so after messing with some design software and showing my work to some friends, they stroked my ego enough and suggested that I should start whoring my design skills out for money. So, there it began.

I spent a marathon week watching a box of VCR tapes on Photoshop 2 and Dreamweaver that I checked out from the library, and a week later I saved up some beer money and sprung for the $25 to buy a business license and presto!

I was an instant, "professional" designer. It was that easy.

I then spent the next six months or so picking up little jobs here and there, mostly from friends who needed cheap design work, as well as some larger jobs from the businesses of some family friends who "let me" do some pro bono work for them in order to beef up my portfolio. (We've all done a few of those, right? Maybe too many?)

As a result, I built up an "ok" basic portfolio, but decent paying gigs were few and far between, and at the time I had no concept of marketing or what it took to land major clients.

That was the year the dot com bubble burst, the "new economy" was going to shit (kind of like now) and major ad and design budgets were dropping like rocks. Needless to say, there was literally no work available for newbie designers. (At least that's what I thought...) I was broke, I had rent to pay, as well as a pile of bills for the loans I took out to pay for my fancy new computer and all my expensive design software, and sadly, my dreams were quickly fading into oblivion.

Instead of quitting though, I decided to dig my heels in, stick with it and after a little bit of creative Googling and Yahooing, I found and placed an ad on an adult jobs message board out of sheer desperation. This was primarily a site looking for adult performers, but there was a little thread for "designers for hire" and to my luck, was empty, so I said, "what the hell" and posted my availability.

My Lucky Break in Porn!

After about a week of waiting, I had almost forgot about the post, when I got an email from an adult webmaster who's wife was a porn star. After a quick phone call, he ended up giving me my first paying adult gig, building some websites for him.

These projects helped me to quickly build a basic adult portfolio, and after that, just from word of mouth referrals from other adult producers and performers, the doors to the adult industry cracked open for me, which, as it turned out, was exploding with opportunity for fast, decent designers.

At that time, while many mainstream companies and investors were going broke, struggling to even explain what the business model for websites, "the internets" new media and e-commerce was all about, adult webmasters were raking in the cash.

It took Amazon a good 10 years before they made a profit. Before Ebay and internet marketing, adult webmasters were doing it from day one. They invented e-commerce, online billing, credit card processing, shopping carts and streaming video on demand. Everyone else just copied what the porn guys were doing.

For a designer at that time, this was an amazing opportunity. It was literally a gold rush of new clients and because of it, there was work everywhere. The trick was, you had to position yourself where the money was, and take chances, so while most designers at that time were sucking up to the mainstream or getting sucked up by Microsoft, I said "fuck it" and jumped head first into porn.

As a result, Devilish Media was born.

Devilish Media

I started Devilish Media as a freelance web and graphic design shop catering to the adult industry and in the beginning, I pretty much took any project that came my way, which was a LOT of them!

The majority of it came from independent adult producers and webmasters, who typically had large databases full of adult content, which they would re-spin into lots of niche based membership websites. These were based on either, the customer demand, or a surplus of available content that they either created themselves or purchased from other adult content suppliers.

Basically a single photoset of two blondes in a lesbian scene could be divided up and spun off into all sorts of different genres of niche websites. Lesbian, blondes, euro, college, MILF, Cougar, coeds, barely legal, dildo/vibrator play, large breasts, small breasts, legs, feet, depending on what they wore (or didn't wear) it could also be heels, feet, shaved, nylon, pantyhose, lipstick, smoking, and the list goes on and on.

At that time, the niches (and design expectations) were pretty basic, top level and straight forward. In the biz it's called "Vanilla Porn", which basically consists of anything softcore, hardcore, blondes, brunettes, redheads, ebony, Asian, lesbian, gay, bondage, blowjobs, cum shots and anal. That was pretty much it, at least on a mainstream, decent sales, decent paying level. (Of course, lots of weird stuff was going on underground, but I'll get to that later on)

Most of these websites were membership tour sites, or affiliate program sites which typically started off with a splash/warning page, then about 3 – 5 long, heavily designed photo or video pages, with previous and next links, and then the final page ending in a sign up form.

I was never much of a coder, so my primary focus was only to do front end design and then chop it up into basic HTML that I would pass on to a developer. The majority of what I did consisted of lots of front end UI for membership sites, banners, photo and video galleries and print ads for the adult industry trade mags and conventions.

I eventually started learning a little bit of Flash, which made me pretty popular with my clients because my rates were still pretty low and a client could get a decent animated banner or header for a decent price. Since I was also a musician, I even offered custom music and audio editing which I would include in the Flash and I even sold a few soundtracks, which ended up in some adult videos.

This went on for a few years. Good, steady & predictable work which paid the rent and built up a pretty decent client base and a decent rep in the industry. I even served as a design moderator on a couple adult forums, (Rated Hot and another one I forgot the name of) which really helped network and get new clients and I met a lot of really cool people in the biz.

All was going great, and then file sharing hit & some pretty crazy new laws were passed and suddenly everything in the adult industry started going to shit.

The Big Shake Up

Right around 2004 – 2005 is when the adult industry suddenly started falling apart. It actually started much earlier, but this is when it started to directly affect me. File sharing and tube sites began to pop up everywhere and started to seriously impact sales on a major level. Most producers were taking a big hit because all of their content was now digital and as a result, being ripped and shared freely all over the net. Lawsuits were flying around like crazy and free porn was everywhere.

People stopped paying for porn & hell needed snow shovels.

Big adult production houses started to either fold or consolidate. Suddenly, the pioneers who invented digital commerce had no clue what to do and as a result, most of the big, "easy money" design projects started to dry up and become harder to find. The outsourcing craze was getting more popular as well, so most of the webmasters who stuck it out started farming the design work to Asia for pennies on the dollar just so they could turn a profit.

In order to make decent money, I had to triple down on lots of lower paying clients. I was working like a dog, around the clock in order to keep up with the joneses. I started burning out because there is only so much time in one day to do quality work, and as a result, started to seriously get concerned about the future of my business and whether or not I should think about taking a new direction, or gasp... getting a real job again.

Right about that time 2 key things happened to me however, that allowed me to say in business and not only survive the downturn in the adult biz, but to take advantage of it and grow beyond my wildest expectations.

Business & Marketing Breakthrough

The first breakthrough was when I made the decision to focus on really taking my business seriously. Having never finished college and primarily relying on my creative talents to get by, it became apparent that unless I learned more about business, sales and money, I would never be able to grow.

As result, I began studying MBA courses, internet marketing, SEO, blogging, economics, investing, personal development. Pretty much anything that might help me optimize and grow my business. I invested a few thousand bucks in online marketing training programs and software, which really helped me to develop some strategies, (which I will discuss in the strategy chapter) that drastically changed my business approach for the better.

Phone Sex & Selling Shovels

The next breakthrough, was when I was contacted by a new client who was a professional phone sex operator, (or PSO as they are called in the biz). She primarily used a phone sex platform called NiteFlirt and I was hired to redesign her listing, which was basically just an HTML page and chunk of simple code, kind of like the old MySpace profiles.

Although I had been working in the adult industry for years, the very secretive world of the phone sex industry was still a big mystery to me and naturally, I jumped at the chance to learn as much about it as possible. What I learned made me see dollar signs! $$$

It turned out that while the big adult production companies were going out of biz struggling to maintain the old digital content business model, the independent adult entertainers and sex workers were growing in numbers and making some decent money.

The shake out of the biz and the struggling economy was creating a lot of desperate, out of work people and phone sex, webcams and dancing was an easy fallback for quick income. The ones who were good at it and smart about it, understood that there was quite a large opportunity to get **clientele who were willing to pay out the nose for unique fantasy experiences.**

While most porn was easily accessible, unique & personalized experiences were not, and **there was quite an affluent market for it.**

Basically, People were getting bored with porn, because there was just so much of it, free online.

Instead, they wanted something unique and phone sex workers were in the prime position to take advantage of this demand and were charging between .99 cents and $20 a MINUTE for it!

Many of theses callers are CEO's, rich and famous celebrities, politicians, clergy, etc. The kind of people who are in the public eye and can't afford to do freaky shit in their real lives, so they pay out the nose to do it in fantasy land over the phone or in a dungeon.

Phone sex operators use a lot of different fake personas for different characters. Often times the voice you speak to on the phone is usually nothing like the real person on the other end. In order to preserve the mystery and protect themselves from discovery by their clients, discretion and secrecy is a must.

Because of this, they conduct a majority of their business related discussion away from the public eye in private, members-only forums. As a result, there is a huge lacking of decent, professional designers, with not only a solid understanding of their special needs, but could also be trusted to participate in the community and respect it's discretionary nature. For me, it was a golden opportunity, so I grabbed it!

In marketing, there is an old saying that goes:

"During a gold rush, the one who makes the most money is not he who digs, but he who sells the shovels."

In my case, the ones digging were the phone sex operators and adult entertainers, and the shovels I sold to them were design, design templates, graphics, sales "tools" and training programs. (but I'm jumping ahead here...)

You see, after my initial client, word of mouth spread and I eventually started to earn a reputation as the "go to guy" for phone sex design work and my business exploded!

Based on this new experience, I was able to not only line up of steady stream of regular clients, but based on their unique needs, I was also able to develop a whole new line of design based products and services that I started selling to them.

These products consisted of pre made templates to decorate their NiteFlirt listings, custom widgets and games to use in their listings and blogs, Wordpress themes, buttons, graphics and even training courses and ebooks to teach them how to use it all.

As the lineup of products grew, as well as the demand for new stuff, I was eventually able to cut way back on designing and focus more on just selling products. This allowed me to raise my design rates significantly, trim out the less desirable and time consuming clients, and only focus on the ones who were cool and could afford what I charged.

After about a year of using this streamlining approach, I was actually able to stop designing completely. Devilish Templates was running basically on autopilot and the money I made from selling products and private consulting made up for what I previously made busting my ass all day doing design.

I have since moved on to become a marketing consultant for major corporations, writing, creating digital products and researching new niches and revenue streams to tap into.

So why am I telling you all of this?

Don't let my exit from being a designer scare you into thinking that the money making potential of the business is tapped out. **On the contrary, there is more opportunity now then ever before if you know how to work it.**

You DO have to be smart about it and learn to apply a system, but the business potential is everywhere.

To be honest, my reasons for getting out of doing adult design are entirely personal.

1. It was never my intention to be an adult designer in the first place, and my goal was always to find some other way to earn a living. It was fun for a while, but it was time to move on. Luckily I was very successful at it and was able to use my experience to evolve into doing something I now really love, which is teaching people like you how to market and grow their businesses. At the root of it, I'm a business man, not a designer.

2. I have a family now and the thought of Photoshopping gaping vaginas in full screen mode with my 3 year old daughter walking around in the room is unacceptable. Time to stop. (If you have kids, this is definitely something for you to consider as well. More on that in a later chapter)

3. With my exit from the biz as a designer, there is NOW A HUGE NEED FOR OTHER DESIGNERS who will cater to my particular niche, which are independent adult entertainers and can provide the quality types of services that I have built a reputation on.

Up until this point, I have been pretty discreet about what I do and who my clients are, mostly out of fear of competition. It is literally a huge untapped niche and I am now offering it up to you on a silver platter, so I would suggest you jump on it while the digital ink you are reading this on is still fresh.

So, with all of that said, enough about me... let's get into what's in it for you!

Shocking Secrets of Adult Design

Chapter 2

The Benefits of Doing Adult Design

As a designer, why should you consider doing adult? Here are the 9 key benefits to consider, that I think are most important.

1. It's Fun!

First off, obviously, if you like porn, (and most people do, whether they admit it or not...) then doing adult design is much more fun than pretty much anything. What other job lets you sit around looking at naked people all day and get paid for it? I think that's a given.

2. Total Freedom

There is nothing much more taboo than sex and nudity, so when designing adult, you pretty much have total freedom. Porn is all about what is eye catching, scandalous, shocking, controversial, intriguing, bold and expressive, so you can pretty much get as crazy as you want (within legal limitations of course). In fact your clients appreciate it.

3. It is Predictable and Therefore, Easily Manageable.

Despite all of the unlimited fetishes, genres, categories and niches you'll be involved with, you're still, basically dealing with images of semi clothed and naked people. In the end, porn is porn, everyone looks the same with their clothes off. The only thing that really changes is the media type and delivery method.

Once you do a few designs, you'll start to see that regardless of the theme and look and feel, you're still dealing with very predictable patterns, shapes and colors. For the most part, your job is to squeeze images of human bodies into collages of various poses into horizontal or vertical boxes, so very quickly you'll discover how easy it is to gage the level of time and difficulty for any type of project.

Tip: This predictability makes it easy to both optimize your time and maximize your rates.

4. Porn is Primarily a Visual Thing

Selling porn is primarily reliant on eye candy. Adult producers rely on constant design and redesign in order to sell their products. As long as they need to sell it, they will need designers to spice it up and make it look good.

5. There is Limited Competition

There are a gazillion designers in the world, but very few are brave enough, smart enough or comfortable enough to do adult design, so the competition tends to be very low. The one's that actually do get involved in adult, are either shit for brains, suck at design, or they rarely stick around more than a year or so because they move on to another mainstream job.

This is the main reason I got started in this business and was able to stay in business for so long. It's a huge untapped resource with constant demand, and very little consistent supply. **The key word being: consistency.**

If you are any good at all, you can pretty much blaze your own trail and count on work always being available.

6. It's The Oldest Profession

They don't call it the oldest profession for nothing. Sex Sells, it always has, it always will. The sex industry has been around since the dawn of man and despite minor ups and downs, it will always be there. Sex and pornography aren't going anywhere, and as long as you're smart about it, you will always have a job in some aspect.

7. B2B is the Key

As an adult designer, you are providing a B2B (business to business) resource. This is the best position to be in because due to the legal, business and moral issues regarding pornography, it will always be in a constant state of change.

Traditional media such as images and video are still around but they are no longer a novelty anymore. Since the demand is low and the market is over saturated, producers are having to evolve and create new technology and experiences.

Being a designer is one of the best places to be right now, because you can both address the needs of the people who are still profiting from the older content as well as make yourself available for people who need design to promote the new forms of content, when they do start to appear. If you have UX, UI, mobile, gaming, app or plugin experience, you are golden.

Adult businesses, content providers and producers will always come and go, because they are the prime targets and are the one's who take the biggest risks, but as a design resource, you can always be there to help address this change with WAY less liability.

8. The Clients are Awesome

I love my clients. They are unique, funny, smart, interesting, honest and open, and due to the personal nature of the content and the work, you will develop a much higher level of trust with your clients than with mainstream clients.

In this industry, since everyone is constantly under fire from all angles, legally, morally and politically, nobody wants trouble, nobody wants to start any shit, nobody wants any unnecessary friction or negative attention drawn to them, so the industry is very good at policing itself and the people as a whole stay pretty mellow.

9. It is Different and Intriguing

If you're a dude, your buddies will think you're the mac daddy. If you are female, your opinions and perspectives on sexuality are invaluable in the industry, and not to mention the guys, will find it intriguing and sexy.

This is a unique job that is unlike anything most people can comprehend. It will open your mind to new ideas and experiences. It will also start some really interesting conversations, which leads me to the next section... and a big question.

Chapter 3

So... do you REALLY want to be an Adult Designer?

It's so funny...

Whenever somebody asks me what I do for a living, I immediately have to size up the poor, unsuspecting recipient to determine if I really want "to go there", because the answer always drops like a bomb and inevitably unleashes any number of typical responses.

People expect you to say " Who me? Oh... i'm a project manager", or "I'm a mortgage broker" blah blah...

Nobody expects you to say "I do porn".

"What do I do for a living? Well, Bob, I design PORN SITES for hookers. OH... sorry if I made you spit V8 juice out your nose, and by the way, I'm engaged to your daughter..." That one just never rolls out right, no matter how you phrase it.

Needless to say, it's a "sensitive" topic that in many situations, justifies discretion, and even a few white lies. If I'm not feeling particularly social, usually I'll keep it simple and safe and just say that I am a designer or a consultant, or even just lie and say I'm a trust fund kid.

Unfortunately, if I go out with friends, one of them will ultimately spill the beans and say something like "Dude... you gotta tell them what you do for a living..." or even worse, "Oh, they know... I already told them. I hope that was ok..."

If I feel brave, bored or obnoxious enough to drop the "porn bomb", and throwing an immediate quirk into an otherwise mundane conversation, there are usually a typical handful of basic "WTF??" reactions.

These are either:

"Noooooo way... are you serious??? That's so cool!"

or sometimes:

"oh..."

(as they turn up their noses, roll their eyes and look the other way with a nauseous expression on their faces...)

Sometimes:

"Wow. Does your mom know you do that?"

(You can also replace mom with: wife, friends, family, boss, kids, church, neighbors, community, etc) Yes, she does, by they way.

This brings me to a question I have for you.

I know you are really excited to get started, but before we dig into all the practical, juicy details, I need to get serious for a minute, because in all good conscious, I first need you to ask yourself some VERY serious questions.

Primarily...

Do you really want to do this?

I know, I know... since you've already purchased this book and are reading this now up to this point, it might sound like one of those "um...yeah, DUH!?" kind of questions, but seriously think about this for a minute before you jump down the rabbit hole.

The most important questions being:

- Do you have any serious moral, emotional or religious reservations that may interfere with you being involved with adult related material?

- Are you comfortable enough with extreme, sexuality explicit topics and content, as a whole, in order to be open minded enough to deal all the various aspects, genres, fetishes, etc. that you will be exposed to in the adult industry? Trust me, it can get pretty weird...

- What would happen if anyone were to find out you run an adult design business? (Be sure to consider your friends, family, children, neighbors, coworkers, social or religious groups, the cop or the church lady next door, etc.)

- Are there any legal restrictions where you live that might interfere with your decision to run an adult design business? Do you even know?

- Are you emotionally, intellectually and financially capable of dealing with the results, should someone find out?

- How good are you at keeping secrets? Can you be trusted with a client's secrets?

- How good at keeping secrets are the people close to you, should they find out that you are an adult designer?

Sorry to piss in your cornflakes here and be a downer, but the fact of the matter is, despite all the recent progress and cultural openness towards sexuality these days, there are still unfortunately, very real, social prejudices that still exist towards people who work in the adult industry.

There are also potentially, very real legal ramifications.

I will go into these in more detail in the chapter: **"Know the Law"**, but for now, just be aware that, in addition to the challenge of applying all the learned skills of design, promotion and marketing, you also need to be hyper vigilant of all the latest legal rulings in order to protect yourself and your livelihood, should they change at a moment's notice. (and believe me, they can and do...)

Being an adult designer and running an adult related business can have many benefits. It can be incredibly fun, it can be entertaining and best of all, it can be lucrative.

However, without a very thorough understanding of just what you are getting yourself into and how to protect yourself, it can be devastating, socially, financially and legally.

So do me a favor and before we move any further, read through that list of questions again and think long and hard about them one more time.

So, can you deal with it? Ok, just checking.

To summarize what you learned in this chapter:

1. Decide if you really want to be an adult designer.
2. Ask yourself some very important questions before you start

Chapter 4

Uncensored Business & Marketing Strategies

"If you don't know where you are going, you might end up somewhere else." – Yogi Berra

In business, having a proper strategy from the very beginning means the difference between success and failure. In this chapter I want to discuss 5 strategies which have been the keys to my success as an adult designer:

These strategies, which I call The Devilish Marketing System ™ are actually fundamental business and marketing strategies. They have helped me to grow my business, to automate, to differentiate myself from the competition and have allowed me to prosper for over 12 years, and through two major economic recessions.

These are universal strategies, meaning that they can be applied, not only to adult, but to any business and will help it to be successful, sustainable and able to grow in all kinds of directions. Learn them, apply them and pass them on.

Avoiding the Money / Time Trap

When you picture where you want to be in the future, where do you see yourself? Do you still want to be photoshopping hardcore, anal sex, cum shots at 70, just to pay the rent?

I'm guessing not, right? I sure don't. Without a strategy however, you might be, because being a freelancer in any business can be a huge trap. I learned this the hard way.

As I mentioned earlier, when I started out, I was broke and desperate. My goal was just to get some design work so I could pay the bills and to create a full time, self employed job for myself.

Well, I succeeded... and I was miserable. Let me tell you why.

If you are just getting started and don't have any clients yet and you really just need to start making some money, it is easy to see how an acceptable goal to shoot for would be to just get to the point where you finally have a steady stream of adult clients and jobs coming in. The rent is getting paid, you have some beer money. Everything is super...

For many people, this, in itself, is quite an achievement. When you first get started, it's a pretty good feeling to finally be self sufficient. A full time porn gig, after all, is pretty cool, and your friends will be jealous as hell!

It wasn't until much later however, when I discovered that unless I came up with a better strategy, I was pretty much going to be stuck doing just that, which was:

Working my ass off 24/7 to stay self employed and just getting by until the next project came along.

Or, as I like to call it:

The Money/Time Trap (aka the Wheel of Doom!)

As you'll discover in later chapters, getting your first jobs and making some money is really the easy part. If you're an "OK" designer, it's really not that difficult to get the ball rolling. The challenge is, what to do AFTER you start getting work, will make the real difference between, a job and a successful business.

There is a common stigma in the adult industry about designers. For the most part they are considered, cheap, slave labor. The faster and cheaper you can crank something out, the better. This is of course a big misconception, since I am living proof, but this kind of thinking is the big trap most newbies fall into. Plus, when the novelty of working with adult content goes away (and it will) it ends up becoming just like any other freelance job.

You see, the biggest problem with being a freelance designer, regardless of the industry, be it adult or mainstream, is that in order to make consistent money, you are pretty much reliant on having to design and be creative all the time.

The challenge with this kind of business model is that there are only so many hours in the day where you can either physically design, or have the creative energy to do so, so at some point, even with a million customers, you start to hit the wall. Or, as I like to call it:

The Wheel of Doom!

Did you ever own a gerbil or a hamster?

If you have, then it probably had one of those wheels in it's cage that it used to run on for hours upon hours, every day.

I had one. My gerbil "Herman" would run and run and run, but the problem with those wheels is that once he got it rolling, he pretty much had to keep running, or else in order to stop, he had to risk getting flipped around about 2 times before the wheel would slow down enough to finally fling himself out of it and crash against the side of the cage.

Being a freelancer is pretty much just like being a gerbil on a wheel.

You run and run and run and chase the "Benjamins", but never really get anywhere.

In this case, "The Wheel" is basically when you reach the maximum capacity of time you can be available to design and the amount of money you can charge for it, because the only way to make MORE MONEY at that point is to have either: MORE YOU, or MORE TIME!

Run Herman, RUN!!!

All of which are impossible, for 3 reasons:

First of all, in order to be the BEST at what you do, YOU ARE the product and the service. You ARE the creative source of what you charge for, so you can't just easily duplicate yourself (unless you have like an identical twin or something...)

Sure, you could always outsource, and i've done it to some extent, however I've found that for what I specialize in, it only works well for certain things.

The main reason is that I base my entire business on doing very specialized work. My clients want MY designs, MY work, MY insider understanding of their needs and MY customer service, not some dude in a third world country, who probably can't even spell "cuckold" or "exophilia" much less understand what it is or all of the subtle, psychological intricacies of the fetish or design style.

Plus, when you are just getting started, you are working with lots of customers with smaller budgets, so you need to stick to tight time boxes in order to be profitable.

In my experience, in order to arrange a quality outsourced project, takes 10 times as much time and energy than if you just cranked it out yourself. The reality is, you really don't save any money, much less the risk of shitty quality work coming back that you have to spend time fixing anyway.

Second, you could always raise your project fees or hourly rates to maximize your time, but this can be very difficult when you are just getting started, because currently, design rates in the industry are very competitive, so you can only charge "so much" to keep new customers interested, at least until you establish a good reputation and can justify higher rates. This of course comes later, but starting out is an uphill battle.

Third, and most importantly, everyone has a life outside of being a designer and nobody should be expected to be in front of the computer staring at a giant hairy vagina, or BBW bukaki burger buffet in full screen, 24 hours a day just to make a living.

What happens when you get sick? Stare at porn all day and you will get sick of it... trust me.

What if you want to take some time off? Stare at that stuff all day and you will need time off...

It's not like a normal job where you get vacation pay, benefits and sick leave... (ok, I guess porn is a benefit... but still...) What happens when you want to sell your business and do something else, but that business relies solely on YOU as the product?

Besides, let's face it, the main reason you are doing all of this in the first place is to stop being a slave to the day job and have MORE FREE TIME and make MORE MONEY, and ENJOY WHAT YOU DO, right?

So, the big question is then, once you've hit "The Wall" and you're riding "the Wheel" at full speed, how can you get off the wheel and still make money?

How can you OPTIMIZE the profit potential of YOU without you needing to be there and spin the wheel all day without having to increase the time and effort it takes to do so?

The answer is simple:

Work at Building a Business, not a Job!

As I mentioned earlier, this book is about what I did to create a successful business. The key word here is to create a business for yourself, NOT a job.

To do this, you have to think outside the designer box just a little bit.

Basically, as a business owner, you've got to make a mental shift from the idea of just running your business as a self employed freelance designer, to instead, build a business that you can one day scale, sell or own passively without you needing to be constantly involved in.

So how do you do this?

Stop thinking like a Designer!

Yes, I did adult design, but I never consider myself a designer. I'm a business man, and I run a business to make a profit to pay the bills, buy the things I want and support my family. It just so happens that one of my strong points is design, and since Adult Design was a profitable, untapped niche, I started off by providing that service, among many other things, for a fee.

In the beginning, on the surface, Devilish Media was just a design firm, however in addition to providing design services, I also created and sold a large number of products and other services. The business eventually grew from just a design firm, to a design and marketing consulting firm, then with the addition of publishing, Devilish Media has grown to be company that sells all kinds of things.

As a result, I have been able to take what I have learned and apply it outside adult. My design business is now just secondary income and basically runs on auto pilot. If I want to take on a special project, I take it, if not, I don't need to.

I did this 2 ways:

1. I built a marketing funnel, as a system for communicating with my clients so I could easily and more effectively engage directly with them and sell them all kinds of things, not just design. I don't need Google. I don't need ads. I have my funnel and I own it.

2. I created a wide spread of products and services that, by selling them, have allowed me to have a secondary source of income, so I didn't HAVE to take every design project that comes down the pipe. I could instead, focus on providing higher quality, more focused service to specific clients and as a result, I could charge MUCH more, and they happily pay it.

Building Your Funnel

The most important aspect of any marketing strategy is the ability to stay in control of your customers, so that you have a reliable way to easily and continuously engage and deliver your sales messages to them.

The easiest way to do that is by building a marketing funnel.

What is a Marketing Funnel?

A marketing funnel is basically a system that I set up on all of my websites, for converting leads (people interested in my services) into recurring jobs and sales. Basically, this works just like a real funnel with the customers falling in the wide top end, and the thin bottom end spits out money and opportunity for me!

The way I do this is by "capturing" contact info of potential customers, who willingly opt in via my mailing list and via social media profiles and posts (Friending, Following, Circling, etc.).

Once this is done, it becomes MUCH easier to deliver sales messages to them, because instead of expending a lot of energy reaching out to customers one at a time with ads or SEO, which are spread out all over the place, expensive and time consuming, I can now deliver targeted sales messages quickly and directly to their inbox with one message, because they are "captured" so to speak, on a list.

While I hate to use the analogy "it's like shooting fish in a barrel" to define this process, that is basically, what it's like.

The Mailing List

The primary way this is done is via a mailing list sign up box, which is located on the sidebar of my portfolio page. Every promotional technique I use online is done with the goal of driving people to sign up to my mailing list.

Here's an example of a mailing list sign up on one of my websites.

How it works:

Potential customers who go to my website are offered incentive to sign up to my mailing list by the promise of a free offer that they can receive in exchange for signing up to my list and giving me their email address.

The free offer is usually something valuable to them, such as free graphics, a coupon for a free banner with every order, or the promise to be eligible for 30% off all design services for as long as they stay signed up. (You can easily offset this to the overall cost estimate, but it still works as incentive)

As soon as they sign up to my list, they are either redirected to the free offer page, or they are sent an email via an auto responder, which contains a link to their downloadable free offer.

Once they are on my mailing list, they are basically "trapped" (of course they can opt out whenever they want) which basically means that they are now guaranteed to receive whatever promotional messages I want to send them. I normally send out at least an email a week to my entire mailing list, and as a result, I get about a 10% –

20% conversion into sales or new jobs or whatever it is I am promoting.

So, basically, any time I want to make some money, need a new project, or have a new product to sell, I fire up an email and I know that everyone on my list will receive the message. I currently have about 3 different adult design related mailing lists, with between 1000 – 3000 targeted, paying adult design customers on each list. At first this might not seem like a lot, but remember that these are pre qualified, targeted buyers.

Here's the basic flow:

Devilish Media's Sinister Funnel of Seduction

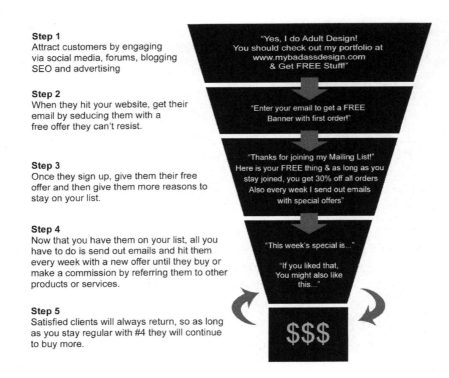

I use my mailing list to either promote my own stuff, or sometimes I make a joint venture partnership with other design related business and promote their stuff to my list in exchange for a percentage of the sales.

These other businesses are made up of a network of adult related businesses that include: copywriters, photographers, hosting companies, affiliate programs, other designers, content providers etc. In return for promoting them, these companies either cut me in for a percentage of the sales for that promotion, or else agree to cross promote me via their mailing lists if they have them.

Your adult list is just a sales channel just like any other. Whatever you can pump into it that will sell, then use it.

Don't Spam

Keep in mind that it is illegal to write spam emails to random people, however since the customer intentionally opts in to the list and clicks the confirmation link in the first email it sends them, you are free and clear to send them as many emails as you think you can get away with and promote whatever you can.

Please Note: I am not a lawyer and this is not legal advice, but due to FTC requirements, you do have to make it very clear in your emails and marketing material what your intentions are as well as giving them the opportunity to opt out whenever they want.

You can read more on the FTC website at:

http://business.ftc.gov/documents/bus71-ftcs-revised-endorsement-guideswhat-people-are-asking

Social Media

The secondary component is to capture leads via connecting on social networks. At the time of this writing, these are forums, Twitter, LinkedIn, Google +, Facebook and Pinterest.

Social media connecting is sort of a "soft funnel" or the large outer ring of the much bigger funnel, so to speak. This is because the messages I send out via social media are usually made with the intention of moving potential customers further into the larger funnel and into my mailing list.

I'll get more into social media later, but for now just be aware that your social channels are the first potential outposts where you can make new customer contact and drive them to your website to join your mailing list.

It is the first outer ring of your marketing funnel, so whenever a new social network shows up that is adult tolerant, I jump on it in order to establish a presence and connect with potential customers.

Become a Premium Service & a Luxury Brand, Immediately!

The way that I have been able to distinguish myself from any competition has been to immediately position myself as a Premium Service provider and a Luxury Brand.

To understand this, let me first give you two example scenarios:

Scenario 1: When a woman walks into the Walmart to buy a pair of flip flops or some beauty products, she most likely has a certain type of service expectation, as well as a price expectation. This is basically poor quality and cheap prices. When she leaves, her feelings reflect her experience. Poor and cheap.

If she walked in and the moisturizing conditioner, which normally was priced at $4.99 was suddenly $500, she would probably need an ambulance from the shock and horror. She would then run out and rage on Facebook to all her friends about how outrageous and how much of a rip off it was.

Scenario 2: When a woman walks into a luxury boutique in Beverly Hills and wants to buy a pair of heels, or to get a full beauty makeover, she also has a certain type of service expectation, as well as a price expectation.

This is basically intensive, one-on-one customer service and outrageous prices. When she leaves, she feels like a million bucks and for that, price was not a concern. Most likely she paid $500 - $2000 for a pair of heels and didn't bat an eyelash. She will then proceed to post a picture on Facebook of her amazing new heels or her beautiful new haircut and will then luxuriate in all of the comments and praise from her jealous friends about how she treated her self. It was "expensive, but oh so worth it!"

Be the Boutique, not the Walmart!

There are a lot of adult design businesses out there, who, unfortunately take their cue from the current hard economic times and try to stay competitive by offering the lowest rates possible to any and all clients who all are:

"on a tight budget but really need this design to be awesome, so I'm hoping you can cut me a deal..." blah blah...

I'm sure you've heard that line before, right? Like, pretty much every client, ever?

In order to maintain these types of rates, these designers either need to work themselves to death, or outsource everything. Both methods do nothing but produce cheap, sub standard, unfocussed work. By doing this, they position themselves for being the "one stop shop" for everything adult design, basically. a Walmart of design.

When I first started in design, I also took this approach. I felt that I had to, in order to stay employed, but I soon discovered that it was unsustainable and I was burning out.

I either needed to change my methods drastically, or quit all together.

The Light Bulb Moment

It wasn't until I started studying marketing and economics that I finally started to understand that I was constantly trying to take the Walmart approach to my business, but my actual strengths were in customer service, knowledge of particular niches and the unique quality of work that I could deliver to my customers.

Applying the Pareto Principle

The Pareto principle (based on Italian economist Vilfredo Pareto) also know as the 80/20 rule, basically states that 80% of the results in anything you do, typically comes from only 20% of your efforts. 80% of your sales comes from 20% of your best clients.

Basically if you trim away 80% of all the useless, time consuming crap that you do every day in your business, including 80% of the leaching, complaining, bargain hunting, time sucking clients, you are left with only needing to optimize for that high performing 20% that will get you the most results (the 80%) and earns you the majority of your money.

The rest of your efforts can then be free to focus on growing and not managing, struggling, putting out fires and pacifying every unnecessary request.

Once I made this discovery, I immediately broke apart my entire business plan, and started to approach everything completely different, as a high priced, luxury boutique instead of a Walmart.

To do this, I took a big gamble by immediately increasing my prices 400% and cutting loose about 50% of my cheap or time consuming clients, in order to focus all of my efforts only on the top clients who paid the most, consistently. I made my availability very scarce and as a result, I only took about 10% of the work that came my way and only if it was perfect for my needs.

This was the right decision to make, however when I first made the switch, it was difficult financially for a while as the shock and awe from the clients that I dropped settled in. It eventually paid off and once the word got out about how difficult to hire, exclusive and expensive I had become, my inbox started filling up with work requests like crazy.

I added immediate value and demand just by adding an additional zero to my prices and wait times.

In retrospect, I should have done this from the beginning, and it took a little time to readjust, however I can't stress how important it is for you to understand this concept and establish this as your way of doing business immediately. It will save you a lot of trouble later.

Focus on Creating Products, Not Services

The next step was to start working on ways to augment my per project income, so I could break away from relying on the need to get paid only for time and services rendered.

To do this, I need to start selling stuff. Selling digital items, to be more specific, that can be created once in a limited amount of time and can then be sold, over and over again, for a decent price. This allowed me to supplement my time-based income by offering things that can continually generate money when I was not working.

Some Product Examples

This course that you are reading right now is part of a wide spread of products and services that I have created to monetize the skills that I gained from doing adult, wrap them up into a re-sellable package and sell them over and over.

Here are some examples of some products that I have created:

The 60 Minute Listing - A lot of my phone sex clients were not so web savvy and lacked basic coding skills to set up a decent NiteFlirt listing using a template.

I create this training course to teach them how to edit HTML code using free tools and software and then post their templates to their account. It includes a video course, a handbook and bunch of HTML templates.

This course still sells like crazy for $79

Flash Quiz Player – A financial domination, multiple choice, quiz game for dominatrixes and PSOs. A lot of my clients were requesting specialized games for their customers to play on a "pay to play" basis, so I developed this Flash quiz game that integrated with their NiteFlirt "pay to view" email service, which they could add to their profiles and blogs.

If the player get's a wrong answer, they have to pay a penalty fee to get an email that contains a special code to go to the next question. If they lose, they have to pay a bigger fee. If they win, they get free content. (or if the Dominatrix is super mean, they "win" the opportunity to pay her more money)

I hired an outsourcer to build this for me and paid about $150. I then made a deal with a well respected copywriter who specializes in PSO and fetish related copy, to write the preloaded fetish quizzes that were included. In exchange for the quiz copy, I agreed to give her business premium exposure on the sales page as well the product documentation, promoting her as a copywriting service who specializes in custom fetish quiz writing.

We then agreed on a joint venture where she promoted the product to her mailing list as well and we split the sales profits.

It sold for:

$75 ea with no quiz content.

$90 ea with a pre written quiz included.

Scrolling Flash PTV Display - My customers needed a way to display lots of items for sale on their NiteFlirt profiles without being restricted to code count limitations. This simple Flash XML feed reader was repurposed so that it could show a lot of items, images and links to the products in order to basically sell lots of stuff like photos, videos, audios, stories, etc.

This product sold for $50 each

Adult is an Untapped Gold Mine

When most people look at the adult biz, they obviously just see what's on the surface: the sex. Basically creating, buying and selling sexually related content and the infrastructure for doing so.

Naturally, you might then assume that the bulk of what you would be designing are adult websites, DVD covers, adult novelty product packaging and all the promotional material that goes along with it, such as banners and print ads, etc.

What most people fail to realize is that the adult industry is an incredible, untapped B2B resource for networking, researching and building new products and services, both adult related and mainstream.

Sex is always in demand, always requiring new and unique products and experiences, and as a result, is in a constant state of innovation.

It is basically a perpetual wild west of opportunity!

Be versatile. It's not just about designing websites. Dig deeper. Anything promotional, social media profiles, mobile apps, games, animation, plug ins, billing platforms, shopping carts, comic books, etc.

If you want to go the product creation route, here is a handful of product ideas:

- Design templates
- Online courses on design, copywriting, SEO, marketing, blogging, how to use Wordpress, how to take better erotic photos, how to set up a webcam, how to record audio, etc.audio, etc.
- Consulting review packages
- Graphics packs

- Erotic book covers, Book cover templates and promotional graphics
- Product packaging templates,
- T-shirts & Stickers, Erotic Calendars, coffee mugs, post cards, etc. Porn starts need SWAG! Make it for them
- 3D models and textures,
- Illustrations & Comics
- Games
- Apps and software to make your customers work easier
- Music production, custom music or sound FX
- Video production
- Photography resources
- Social media profile pimpage
- Kindle formatting for erotic books
- Sharable social MEME images with custom URL's

Tip: Pay close attention to the fetish section to get more ideas how to think outside the box.

As we move forward, I want you to stop thinking of yourselves as just a designer, who's sole purpose is to provide design services to people in the adult industry.

Instead, I want you to think of yourself as someone who is using design as a way to lean more about what people in the adult industry want, and then use your design skills and your new found business and marketing savvy to provide that.

There are a ton of different ways to make money as a designer simply by providing mainstream types of services and reworking them to fit adult needs.

Again, **work at designing a business for yourself, not a job.**

If you apply these strategies up front, it will save you a lot of time, a lot of money and you will always be ahead of the competition.

So to summarize what you learned in this chapter:

1. Avoid the Money/Time Trap
2. Work at building a business, not a job.
3. Establish a Marketing Funnel Immediately
4. Provide a Premium Service & Charge Premium Rates
5. Focus on creating unique re-sellable products, not time based services

Chapter 5

A Typical Day, Designing Porn

Here's a peek at what a typical day on the job as an adult designer might include. It's also another little test to see if you have the cojones to deal with it.

(This is all true stuff by the way...)

- Wake up, make a coffee, make a bowl of lucky charms (my fav), flip on the computer, consider putting on pants, and try to forget the fucked up dreams I had last night because this job will seriously mess with your head (and your sex life) if you let it.

- Check Twitter and then scan the adult message boards looking for news, legal updates and new product ideas, and trying to ignore all the posts from people complaining about how "the adult industry is dead, file sharing destroyed the biz and there are no customers and no money being made anymore".

- Check my overflowing email inbox with 2 pages full of new customer emails. Paying customers with money. (Wait... the industry was dead right?)

- Write back about half of them to tell them that I am too busy to take their project.

- I'll confess that most of the time this is because their content is either too boring, poor quality, uninspiring or honestly, sometimes they are just too damn ugly or freaky for me to tolerate having to stare at their weird, naked asses all day.

Seriously, I don't do this to be mean. It's just that if a project is uninspiring, I can't do my best work, and if I can't guarantee a good service, I won't take the job.

Adult is all about fetishes, and these demand a large understanding of it's psychology. If, for some reason, I can't grasp whatever weird, freaky, shit the client's fetish is all about, I also won't feel comfortable that I would do a good job, so I'll pass on it.

Sometimes, I simply just don't need the extra work. I actually refer out more work to other designers than I take in.

- Get pinged on ICQ by a certain porn star about a project and politely have to remind a her, yet again, that "No, I won't accept sex in trade for design work the next time I'm in LA"

- Answer back a client to tell them that I think the orange logo makes their new cum shot website look much more "professional" than the green one.

- Take 10 minutes to write an email and send it to my mailing list of targeted niche based clients, announcing some new products and a limited time only sale on something.

- Go to the coffee shop and write another chapter for my next book

- Finish checking my inbox and make a "cha-ching!" noise for every time I see a new "You've made a sale" or "You've got Money!" or "Payment Notification" emails roll in, as a result of that 10 minute email I sent out.

Shocking Secrets of Adult Design

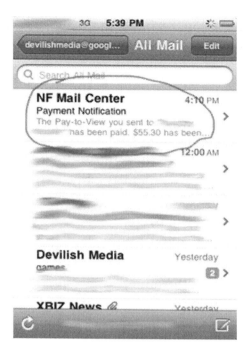

- Click a single button that makes a Photoshop filter add a hazy, Vaseline lens style pornographic glow effect around a folder full of euro hotties images.

  Then bill it out at top dollar as a special service called Pornification ™.

  (Note: I won't even lift a finger to click the Photoshop icon to open the program for less than $200, that's how I roll...)

- Try not to think about spending the next hour in full screen mode, having to do any of the following:

  1. Photoshopping out some accidental, unsightly pieces of shit that showed up on a guy's dick in a series of anal sex photos, because the "recipient" of said acts didn't bother to use an enema properly before the shoot. Messy...

  2. Trying to figure out exactly what the client means by "Can you do something to make her pussy look less old?"

regarding a certain set of photos and then, just what exactly to do about it.

Tip: The blur and smooth tools are your friends.

3. Removing the pimples, varicose veins and junkie track marks on the inner thigh of a model for a client who wants to use the content for a "hot babes" website.

4. Retouch a series of photos of a famous porn star, in order to slim down her waist because she's worried that she is starting to show that she is pregnant.

5. Retouch a series of foot fetish pics because the model had a bad case of greenish-white athlete's foot fungus that showed in the photos.

- Politely remind a certain phone sex worker client, yet again, that "no, I won't accept phone sex calls in trade for design work"…

- Respond to the email from a dominatrix who's name starts with Mistress/Princess/Goddess/Baroness/Seductress/whatever and try to remember if she is a new client or an old client who's name also starts with mistress,/princess/goddess/seductress/humiliatrix, Whatever… (I mix this up like, once a week… seriously, they need a new angle.)

- Send some text off to another professional phone sex operator client so she can record some sexy audio for a mainstream multi-million dollar real estate video project, a video game and another project to promote a religious book.

- Charge a certain politician to update a single line of text on a graphic for his secret "Dungeon" forum and then touch up one of his kid's baby photos so he can mail them out as Christmas presents to the family.

- Turn down a project to design a website for these old dudes who dress up like elves and then use needles to inject saline solution IV's into their scrotums in order to inflate them like water balloons and then dance around the room in their tights and shoot videos of it.

  I give them credit for trying to monetize by upselling medical equipment from their website, but still.... (I warned you about the messed up dreams...I think I'm scarred for life from that one...)

- Ignore and delete about 5 emails from desperate, ignorant, illiterate, dumbasses, who write things like:

  "Dear sir, I wanna hire you ter make mah pern website. I need it done by tomorrow and it needs ta be preefessional looking. I got 2 days to pay the rent or they gonna take my big screen TV and my 4 kids. I am writing you from rehab and I don't know what fer and mah baby daddy took this nekkid picture of me from his phone. How do I get it on mah compooter...? I only got $20 dollars but I aint got no credit card... maybe you can call me and spend the next 5 hours of yer valuble time helping me figure out how ta change the batteries in mah remote?" (I'm not exaggerating...)

- Charge a client to spend the entire day logged in to one of the hundreds of adult websites that I get FREE access to, in order to go through and review 100's of gigs of super hot porn content for a major client's next new website. Yep, it's tough...

- Plan my next trip to the any one of the adult industry expos that happen every year, so you can meet more clients, meet porn stars and go to parties where all kinds of super crazy shit happens.

Chapter 6

The Adult Industry

Based on a 2010 statistics report (for 2006), there is over $100 Billion in estimated global sales revenue being made annually from adult related businesses.

It claims that the porn industry in the USA made about $13 Billion in annual sales revenues. China has the highest Porn Sales Revenues at $27 Billion, followed by South Korea ($25 Billion), Japan ($19 Billion) then the USA.

According to a 2006 article on Xbiz:

"China is the world's largest exporter of sex toys and novelties, with an estimated 1,000 factories involved in the manufacture of "adult healthcare products." The Chinese government estimates that about one-third of all adult products and 80 percent of sex toys and condoms sold worldwide are made in China, with annual revenues from sales of Chinese adult products reaching RenMinBi 50 billion ($6.7 billion)."

Interestingly enough, South Korea is said to have the highest per capita (per person) spending rate on porn, which averages out to an amazing $526 per person! WOW! Korea, that's a lot of porn??

The Bad News

The most recent report from Xbiz (in 2012 at the time of this writing) states that it is now estimated that adult industry gross revenues are now within the $5 billion-plus range worldwide.

So, somehow we went from $100 Billion to $5 Billion in just 2 years? All because of file sharing? If so, those are some unbelievable, radical numbers.

What I take from this is, basically, if you put all your ducks into a digital content model these days, you're going to get screwed. As an adult producer, if you didn't see that coming a mile away from the first day you learned that you could burn a movie to a DVD to infinite, well... surprise.

The Good News

Now, I have no way of knowing how factual any of these statistics are past or present, however I'm going to make an assumption that NONE of them are accurate.

They simply do not take into account all of the businesses that are either mainstream but have some adult related business connection (like Amazon selling vibrators renamed as therapeutic massagers, handcuffs, condoms, costumes, sexy underwear, thumbscrews, dog collars, feather dusters, ten penny nails, trash bags, joy gel, fish hooks, duct tape, plastic wrap, etc) nor all of the bazillions of dollars in under the table money made by prostitution, phone sex, secret dungeons, swinger clubs, strip clubs, massage parlors, etc.

It's kind of like trying to put a monetary figure on the drug industry. I've personally know strippers who bring home between $200 - $1000 a night in tips! And they were the honest ones who actually claimed all of that. Of course, those tips then went to support the drug industry, but that's... another story...

The reality is, trying to put a dollar amount on human sexuality is impossible, because it covers so many areas and has touch points in so many industries, products, services and aspects of human behavior. Just like the drug industry, due to it's discretionary nature, there is so much unreported activity, that we can only skim the surface to make any kind of real monetary estimate.

In the chapter Niches & Fetishes, I will dig much deeper into some specialized areas of the adult biz and how you as a designer can both identify and profit from them, however for now, just be aware that basically, any product or service involving sex or sexuality could be considered part of the adult industry.

Seriously, ANYTHING, and NOT just the small, generic pieces of the gloom and doom pie charts that keeps getting passed around lately by the ones grasping to the last threads of a digital content model.

As you take the next step to familiarize yourself with what is technically considered the "adult industry" at least (as far as most people tend to think of it) try to keep an open mind and think in broader terms. It will open up a much larger set of opportunities for you later.

Learn the Biz

The first thing you need to do, obviously, is to familiarize yourself with the "Adult Industry" as a whole, in order to get a feel for who these whales are, what their businesses are and what kind of design services they need the most.

While there are many similarities between mainstream and adult from a purely business perspective, due to all the legal issues, there are some rather unique challenges which effect the way that business is done.

I could write a whole book on the Adult Industry itself, but since it is constantly changing, the best places to learn with the most up to date info are already online and freely accessible.

A few, excellent, very reputable trade resources I recommend for getting started and learning the biz are as follows. There are more listed in the Resource Chapter at the end of this book, but these are the biggies.

Xbiz

Xbiz is the leading adult industry trade magazine in the USA.

http://www.xbiz.com

Be sure to sign up to Xbiz.net, their social network for adult industry professionals and join in on the discussions

http://www.xbiz.net

I also recommend signing up for the Xbiz Monthly Magazine. You can either read it online or order the print version for free and they will mail it to you every month.

http://www.xbizdigital.com/

AVN Online

http://www.avn.com/

The following are adult webmaster forums that have been around a while and are full of knowledgeable industry professionals.

Cozy Frog

Cozy Frog is a great beginners resource with a lot of useful information http://www.cozyfrog.com/

Cozy Academy has a good set of overview articles and a glossary that will at least get you started with the basics:

http://www.cozyfrog.com/academy/index.aspx

GFY

http://www.gofuckyourself.com/

YNOT

http://www.ynot.com/

Medium Pimpin

http://bbs.mediumpimpin.com/

What To Look For? Potential Annual and Lifetime Value

The way to approach researching the industry, is to try to identify new clients or areas of interest based on what you think is their potential **Annual and Lifetime Value.**

Based on my experience, as well as a few informal polls I conducted with the help of some leading industry producers, affiliates, etc, I was able to determine that the average "successful" adult business* will usually spend anywhere from between $2k to $100k per year, on design.

note that these figures are based on the businesses that hire out for design and not the ones who have internal designers

While this seems like a wide spread, what this means is that there is between $2k and $100k in potential income for YOU per client, per year. It is important to start to think of new business opportunities based the annual spending and the lifetime value of a client instead of just a per project rate.

Don't think of a client as "this guy is usually good for a couple banners once a year" but instead, think of him as "what do I have to do to secure the $50k total he normally spends per year on design". Then focus on what you can do to secure that spending.

The trick is to figure out which clients are the whales, i.e. which ones spend the most on design, per project and position yourself to be the most likely candidate for that work and that cash

Things to learn and pay close attention to:

- Get an understanding of the basic lingo and how things work, what is new tech, what is old tech, what is popular, what is not, etc.

- What are galleries, link lists, membership sites, VOD, TGPs, MGPS, turnkeys, video sites, tube sites, cam sites, phone sex sites, dating sites, blogs, mobile sites, affiliate programs, online shops, social media profiles, etc. As a designer, you probably know a lot of this already, but if not, check them out.

- What, out of all of that is being used currently, what is not? What works, what doesn't?

- What software, platforms, applications and content management systems are people using to plug it all together?

- What billing systems are people using, so you know how they make their money?

- What is B2C (customer facing)? What are the B2B (Business to Business) services?

- How are all of these things being used in the Adult Industry that may be different or similar than how they are used in mainstream?

- Get to know people and their prospective businesses. Who will be wanting to hire a designer and more likely to pay you for your services?

- Who are the photographers, the performers, actors/actresses and models, producers, escorts, content providers, the traffic specialists, the other designers, the webmasters, the hosting providers, the affiliate managers, the copywriters, the forum moderators, etc?

- Who are in large companies who would hire you for large projects? Who are independents that might need a lot of small projects?

- What are the problems that people are facing that you can solve with your skills?

- What are the complaints that they have that you can help with?

- In comparison to all of this, what strengths do you have from being a mainstream designer that you can bring to the table to provide value for your new potential adult clients?

- What weaknesses do you have that might need addressed?

- Where is the money being made? Where is it not?

- What are the laws and legal limitations and ramifications to everything listed above? (Be sure to read the next chapter, Learn the Law. VERY IMPORTANT!)

I know that this a lot to learn, but the good news is, because of the nature of the industry, ALL of that is in a constant state of change and therefore, all of that needs designers like you on a regular basis to help with the changes and to meet the new needs, as they come up.

The more you learn about adult industry and how it all works, the more opportunities you will have

So to summarize what you learned in this chapter:

1. Learn the biz
2. Learn to identify potential clients and where the potential is for revenue.

Chapter 7

Know the Law

You need to pay very close attention to this chapter, because the most important advice I can offer you in this entire book is this:

Make it a regular practice to CONSTANTLY pay attention to, be aware of and have a solid understanding of the most current laws, regulations, legal limitations and ramifications of being involved in the Adult Industry.

Please note that I am not a lawyer, so I am in no way able to provide real legal advice, but trust me when I say that you NEED to know this stuff and take it very seriously. Why?

It Will Save Your Ass and Keep You Out of Jail!

New laws are constantly changing and being passed that drastically effect what you can and can't do in the adult industry, and so you must make it a number one priority to stay informed of these, at all times.

Sometimes these laws happen at a local level in your neighborhood, town or city, sometimes on a state or regional level, sometimes on a national level, sometimes in other countries, but the result usually filters down to the entire industry and eventually, it effects everyone.

It effects the work you do for your clients, what types of work you accept, what you display on your portfolio and/or the products and services you might offer.

Knowing the Law Makes You a Valuable Asset

The good news is, the more you know and stay up to date with all of the legal requirements regarding the adult industry, the more valuable you become to your clients.

For the clients that are aware of current laws and regulations, you become a trusted asset, because you understand their needs and can apply it to their projects without the need for lots of explanation.

For the ones who maybe aren't up to speed, and there are many, you also become a valuable, trusted asset, because your knowledge and consulting can and will save their asses. Regardless, this also helps to support you being able to charge a premium rate for your expertise.

Legal Resources

The following are some good starter resources for you to get a proper understanding of the current laws. I suggest you spend a fairly decent amount of focused time going through this and take a lot of notes if you need to.

If you have questions, and you probably will, there will be more resources in the following chapters where you can network and ask questions from industry people who have first hand knowledge of how all of this will affect you.

If you have access to a Lawyer or legal council, it wouldn't hurt to discuss this with them as well.

Legal Primer

http://www.cozyfrog.com/academy/09-legal-primer.aspx

What is 2257?

http://www.law.cornell.edu/uscode/html/uscode18/usc_sec_18_0000 2257----000-.html

XXXLaw

http://xxxlaw.net/

Xbiz Legal

http://www.xbiz.com/news/legal

Some Tips for Designers

Now that you've had a chance to go over some of that scary stuff, here are some tips and rules of thumb that I always stick to, just to cover my ass.

Again, this is not legal advice, because if someone really wants to nail you for something, they will find a way to do it. Doing the following though, just helps to stay low on the proverbial radar, and as a result, stay in business, stay professional and out of jail.

Obscenity Laws

Obscenity laws change like the weather. The definition of obscenity also changes depending on who you ask, and what the culture is where they live.

According to the Oxford dictionary, the difference between pornography and obscenity is as follows:

- Pornography: printed or visual material containing the explicit description or display of sexual organs or activity, intended to stimulate sexual excitement.

- Obscene: offensive or disgusting by accepted standards of morality and decency, offending against moral principles; repulsive, repugnant:

The problem, at least in the USA, is that while pornography is generally not considered illegal, once it can be deemed obscene, it then becomes illegal.

As you can see, this gets complicated and is very subjective, so this is how I approach it.

As a rule of thumb, if it is something that you see on normal, national TV or on a non adult magazine cover at a major news stand where your address of business is, it is generally "ok" and falls within the boundaries of not obscene.

- In some parts of the Middle East and Asia, however, sometimes this means anything other than eyes that isn't covered can be considered obscene.

- In the USA, this usually means non see-through swimsuits and underwear is the limit. Basically no body fluid, genitalia, or nipple showing.

- In Europe, they are much more relaxed about this. Full frontal nudity is on prime time, TV commercials and the front page of the daily paper, so again, this is relevant to where you live.

Since my primary place of business is in the USA, I go with the "norm" in the USA and just assume that anything that is considered nude or pornography in the USA has the potential to be classified as obscene and therefore "could be" considered illegal by someone.

So if all nudity can technically be considered obscene, how are you supposed to show off your work? Simple.

Don't show any nudity on your portfolio

Now, you and I both know that as an adult designer, you are going to be designing all kinds of things that fall far beyond the realms of what is able to be defined as pornography or obscene. It wouldn't be porn if it weren't risqué or taboo, and since designing it is your business, you of course want to be able to show off your work.

Be careful however, not to lose sight of the fact that **you are first and foremost a designer and you are selling your design skills, not porn,** so as a rule of thumb, leave it to your customers to show all the nudity in their products and services. Let THEM take the hit for it, should it be deemed obscene.

I'll confess that I used to display ALL of my work in it's hardcore entirety, however, over time I got to the point where I stopped showing nudity in my online portfolio. Now, if I want to feature a screenshot of a website I did for a client, I will go and put stars or hearts or blur over all of the naughty bits.

Keep in mind that a potential client looking at your portfolio will be looking at your design sensibilities. They could give a crap about how much nudity is being shown in the screenshots. Chances are they see enough nudity as it is, that they might even welcome not having to see it anyway.

My motto is: When in doubt, leave it out.

If you even have the suspicion that something is too naughty to show, don't show it or at least put stars over it. Don't take any chances. It's not worth it, and it wont hurt your design credibility.

Section 2257 Disclosures

In compliance with Title 18 of the United States Code. Section 2257, ALL producers and secondary producers (webmasters and content providers) are required to have documented proof of age of ALL models for every piece of adult oriented content that they show.

They are also required to post a prominently displayed compliance statement on their website stating that the website complies with these requirements.

As a designer, this puts you in a crappy place because, while you want to display your hottest work on your portfolio, you don't really want to go through all the hassle and be responsible for ALSO having to maintain legal records for every model from every client, in every one of your designs.

Unfortunately, technically and legally, even though you are way lower on the radar than the clients who own the adult websites where this content is featured, you still are required to keep records and post a compliance statement as well, because by posting any kind of adult related content in your portfolio, you also fall under the category of a secondary producer.

Typically this compliance statement is added to a separate page on your portfolio named "2257". You can place the link to this in your footer, so while it is easy to find for anyone looking for it, it doesn't take up a prominent place in your navigation or other precious real estate on your site.

A completely legal compliance notice should ideally be written by a lawyer, however if you check any adult website, they all typically say about the same thing, so you can basically piece your own together.

Most of compliance statements typically say something to the effect of:

18 U.S.C. 2257 Record-Keeping Requirements Compliance statement

All models, actors, actresses and other persons that appear in any visual depiction of actual or simulated sexual conduct appearing or otherwise contained in or on yourdomain.com were over the age of eighteen (18) years at the time of the creation of such depictions.

This Web site complies with all Federal statues and regulations. (18 U.S.C 2257 and CFR 75)

Records are available for inspection during normal business hours. or in accordance with federal labeling and record keeping laws (18 U.S.C. 2257 and CFR 75) The records required by Federal law for this Web site are kept on file with.

Your Name Business Name Your Address

Basically this just states that you are acknowledging that all of the content on your portfolio features models who are 18 or over. It also says that if for some reason, you are called into question regarding a model featured in your portfolio who is under question of being under 18, you provide an address where you keep this info in order to be able to show the proof of age documentation proving that they are, in fact 18.

Yep, it sucks... but that's the law currently, so it must be followed. If you are worried about your address showing up in searches, at least add a no follow script on that page, so anyone Googling your name wont see it, but still... it's gotta be there on your site somewhere.

Because of all of this, you can now understand why I make a point of not featuring any nudity in my portfolio. It makes you much less of a target. Of course, it won't cover your ass entirely because weird stuff can happen, but again, it insures that you are way low on the radar. Again, I am not a lawyer so this is not legal advice, so if you have any questions at all about this, you should really consult one.

As annoying as this is however, it also forces you to pay much closer attention to the content your clients are giving you. Because of this:

Know your clients & where they get their content!

Usually as long as you know your clients and trust that they are aware of the laws and follow them, they will always have proof of age docs for all of their stuff. They HAVE to, and if they know what they are doing, they will include it when sending you design content. Remember, all adult content that you purchase must have this info included.

So, even if someone really wants to track you down for an image of a model that was nude, but is now non nude, because you covered up the naughty bits, and STILL wants to get proof of age and for some reason you don't have it, you should still be able to track it down from your clients pretty darn fast.

You'll also start to recognize models that you know are of age because you've worked with their content before, so you'll start to get a feel for what is safe and what is questionable.

I have turned down several projects, however, entirely on a hunch that that particular client was too much of a shit for brains to know and understand these laws, had no proof of age, and probably either picked up the content from a disreputable place, or doesn't even know where it came from.

DO NOT take that chance. If you even get the slightest hint of a gut feeling that the content is non compliant, don't take the project.

Don't be stupid! Know the law, stay legal and stay out of jail!

So to summarize:

1. Knowing the Law. It will save your ass and make you a valuable asset
2. Don't show any nudity on your portfolio. When it doubt, leave it out!
3. Learn, follow and be compliant of Section 2257 Disclosures
4. Know your clients & where they get their content!
5. Don't be stupid. Stay out of Jail.

Now, let's get into the weird stuff!

Chapter 8

Niches and Fetishes

You've probably heard the statement that "sex sells", but what does that really mean? What we should be asking is:

- What kind of sex sells?
- Who is selling it?
- Who is buying it?
- & how much are they willing to pay for it?

Have you ever heard the phrase that there are riches in niches? Well, it is 100% true! In adult, picking the right niche is very important.

A niche is a term for describing any kind of subset of an existing market. In his book "The Long Tail", author Chris Anderson talks about how we are quickly moving to a specialization economy. The more unique, obscure, and specialized a product or service is, the more value it has.

Once you go down the long tail far enough, your niche jumps to sub niche, and then to micro niche, which is where the untapped, hyper specialized markets can be found and monetized.

In adult, a micro niche is basically just another word for a fetish. In other words:

It means that people are into ALL KINDS of weird & kinky shit

that they are willing to pay decent money for!

The weirder their fetishes are, the more they are willing to pay top dollar for your clients to address their unique needs, to provide products and services based around them as well as to be discreet about them.

Example:

I ran an adult design business (niche) designing NiteFlirt listings and templates for dominatrixes and phone sex workers (sub niche) who specialize in customers into cuckolding, forced intoxication, financial domination and blackmail (micro niche, aka fetishes).

Typically, the more obscure a fetish is, the more your clients will be able to charge for it, and so you in turn, can charge them higher for your specialized knowledge and the ability to design their stuff base on that knowledge.

So what exactly is a Fetish?

A fetish is normally defined as a sexual connection to a specific type of object or activity. It can be a subtle thing or an obvious thing. Sometimes it's not as easily defined as a typical sexual attraction or type of sex act.

Sometimes it's a neurosis, sometimes it's a religion, often times, it's a lifestyle with it's own economy and community.

Ideally, these are what you are looking for because people who are willing to base their entire lives around their fetishes will spend money at any cost to maintain them.

Hidden Niches = Hidden Clients = Hidden Opportunities

Once you understand the unique, psychological aspects and behaviors of a particular fetish, the more you will find ways to, not only optimize your designs for it, but to identify additional revenue streams that may be connected to them.

Here's an example:

My phone sex and dominatrix clients do a lot of dominant/submissive role play with their customers.

In dominant role play, something as subtle as the copy text capitalization of words such as, you/You, he/He, she/She or me/Me are vital details to fitting the role. By learning these little details, I was able to add specialized copywriting services in addition to design and as a result was able to charge a premium rate for this specialized knowledge.

Having this kind of deeper understanding of a fetish not only immediately adds instant value to the quality of your services, it also offers you the opportunity to educate your customers about these types of things, which also adds to your value as a consultant.

I would suggest studying as much as you can about the fetishes and niches you choose to cover. The subject matter might be difficult to stomach sometimes, however it will make all the difference in the world to your customers, and they will recognize this and pay you well for it.

Dig Deep, Go Spelunking

People feed their fetish desires in all kinds of ways. The sex industry is so much more than just porn videos and websites. As a designer, you'll have a lot of opportunities to design all kinds of things.

The trick is to figure out what people are into and what they are willing to pay for it, and then how you can use your design skills and your newly educated business and marketing brain to take advantage of what you discover.

In order to do that, you've got to think outside the box. You've got to go spelunking.

Spelunking is what they call people who explore caves and underground passages. I like to call it that because in order to do fetish research, I spend a large majority of my time online digging through the deepest darkest corners of the internet and exploring the murky depths of psychology and human sexuality.

I read a lot of strange stuff. I spend a lot of time playing undercover and browsing obscure chat rooms, social networks, groups and forums, asking questions and getting freaky answers. Let me tell you, I've seen a LOT of weird stuff and I've chatted to a lot of different kinds of people into all kinds of different things.

Sometimes you discover whole hidden communities and micro economies based around some of the most simple things.

Let's take lipstick, for example.

Check out: http://www.lipstickfetish.org

This is a whole forum full of people (men and women) who are totally into lipstick.

If you dig deeper, there are sub categories for lipstick images, how to do awesome lipstick effects in Photoshop, lipstick stories, lipstick porn, lipstick tips for guys and TV/TS, lipstick art, celebrity lipstick fan sites, it goes on and on.

If you have decent photo retouching skills, here is a prime location for making yourself and your services known. You could literally be a rock star in the makeup fetish world. Sure, maybe there aren't enough potential customers there to live off of, but I'd be willing to bet you could easily scoop up a few "long terms" to throw on the client heap.

You could offer design services to people with lipstick porn sites, or better yet, offer courses in photo retouching. If you look around on that forum, you might even find some people with more skills then you have and you might even learn a thing or two. I did ;)

What to look for in a profitable Niche/Fetish

When you stumble across one of these hidden, micro economy based niche/fetishes, try to look for some key signs that your design services could be in demand:

- Are there affluent people there?
- What are they buying?
- Are there any businesses based around this niche/fetishes?
- What are they selling?
- What are the challenges these businesses are having, in either selling, promoting or setting up a website to sell their stuff. Would they need a designer?
- Are these businesses promoting their businesses with specialized ads, banners or graphics?
- Where are they getting the content for these fetishes and who are the ones selling it?
- Is the quality of the design good or bad?
- Are there other designers there?
- If so, do they suck and can you drop in and crush the competition with our mad design skills?
- If there is business to be had there for you, can you promote that work on your portfolio?
- Is there enough of a demand to benefit from having a more targeted mini portfolio to only promote services for that niche/fetish?
- Are there any skills you've picked up from other niches/fetishes/mainstream that are needed and lacking in

this new niche/fetish community that you can repurpose and offer up to meet these demands?
- If so, can you get away with charging double or triple for it?

If any of these things exist there, you know you've probably found a little potential gold mine. If not, then keep digging. These kinds of communities are where your competitive advantage comes from, so always be on the lookout for them.

Classifying Fetishes

Sometimes you discover more than you can handle. There really are no limits to the obsessive nature of the human mind, so a lot of what I find is just TMI (too much information)

As a general rule of thumb, if it is legal and consensual, it is within the realm of fair game, however, if a fetish or it's content makes me want to take a shower just by thinking about it, I'll usually pass, should the opportunity present itself and a client comes along.

I tend to classify fetishes into 3 basic levels of tolerance.

Vanilla Fetishes - Examples: basic sex. straight, gay, lesbian, bisexual, redhead, brunette, blonde, Asian, ebony, Latin, light bondage, blow jobs, hand jobs, body builders, pantyhose, heels, feet, fat, anal, ugly, trannies, lady boys, hermaphrodites, pop shots, gang bangs, interracial, cougar, MILF, etc. Basic, run of the mill stuff.

Freaky Fetishes - Examples: cuckolding, giantism, chastity, piercing, stomping, smothering, asphyxiation, forced intoxication, robot talking, spitting, pissing, diapers, blackmail, flogging, blood drinking, balloon popping, nail scratching, fart sniffing, cosplay, gloryholes, sneezing, sleeping, snoring, amputees, train fuckers, electrocution, fucking machines, etc.

Shit Eaters - This includes animal fuckers, self mutilation, rape or worse - These should be self explanatory and not worth discussing. It's the line I don't cross and I want nothing to do with. I think you can probably imagine where they end, so if you want my advice, just stay away from them and don't even go looking. Be smart, stay out of jail and your conscious will thank you for it later. Enough said?

I Prefer Not to Go There – There are also some "vanilla" themes that I also stay far away from. Any projects involving topics such as barely legal, young, virgin or teen, among a few, are a no go for me, purely because of the implied underage meaning behind it.

Remember: If you have even the slightest suspicions about the possibility of content featuring under aged models, don't hesitate to ask to see the client's 2257 docs for all of the content before taking on any work. Better safe than sorry.

You can always say No

As I mentioned before, you will be looking at this stuff all day and it can start to really effect you, emotionally. If you can handle it, there is a lot of money in those weird little things, but again, it really boils down to what you can tolerate.

Sometimes the money just isn't worth the pain and effort. Not only is it a personal preference thing, it is also a customer service issue.

Basically, if you're not "into" what you are designing, you can't insure you will produce quality work, so if something is just way too far out there for you, it is better to just pass, in order to focus on something you know you can nail. The money is not worth it and the time you waste not hitting the mark could be spent elsewhere on another more productive project.

Where to look for Fetishes

So where do you go to research and get ideas for niches & fetish?

Looking past just going Google and typing in "weird, freaky fetishes" here are some places to start.

Kink Bomb

http://www.kinkbomb.com/categorylist.php

Kink Bomb is an adult video site that features a whole universe of micro niche/fetish based videos. This is an excellent place to discover what entertainers and cam performers are learning about their customers and then creating mini products related to them. It is also a great place to scope out perspective new clients in need of your services.

The last time I checked, they had a huge list of fetishes that they have categories for. If you are looking for keywords for targeting SEO on your portfolio or to offer as a service, their list is pretty comprehensive.

Medical

There is a large need for adult services that cater to health problems or to people who are handicapped, to seniors, etc. Basically, people who will pay for convenience and discretion. This also creates fetishes. Medial equipment, wheelchairs, amputees, casts, nurse and doctor play, etc. (remember the testicle inflation elves...)

There is not only a large untapped demand for design, but also User Experience design to help meet the challenging needs.

Poser & 3D Erotic Art

There is a huge fan base of people into 3D erotic art. Both people who like to look at it, and the people who like to create it. 3D Art, 3D software, models & textures are a huge growing market, both mainstream and adult.

Renderosity is a HUGE micro economy of 3D artists and fans. Lots of fetish stuff there.

Check out http://www.renderosity.com

SynfulMindz is another 3D site and forum based entirely around fetish related 3D models. Basically, whips, chains, spikes and latex clothing for 3D characters.

Check out: http://www.synfulmindz.com

In regards to 3D, a lot of models are getting paid to have their nude bodies scanned to create original 3D characters and textures. A designer with decent 3D and Photoshop skills could find a lot of opportunity here. I also think porn stars especially, should consider jumping on this trend from a branding perspective.

Erotic Art

DeviantArt is FULL of erotic art and as well as a great place to network with other artists, designers and photographers. You'll find lot's of art porn here as well as a ton of people who need websites to showcase their work.

http://www.deviantart.com/

Trendwatcher Sex - Trendhunter sex is always a good place for new crazy ideas that easily cross over to mainstream.

http://www.trendhunter.com/cool-hunting/category/Naughty-Trends

Erotica Writers Forums and Groups

People who write erotica can come up with some pretty twisted stuff. Check out the erotic stories sites:

http://www.literotica.com

Erotic authors are constantly needing people to design their book covers, so I think this is a huge untapped niche that I have yet to explore in a lot of detail. They also need blogs, so if you have Wordpress skills, here is a prime market.

Magazine Racks

Some of my favorite magazines for design ideas and trends are: Bizarre Magazine, Inked, Alternative Press, Skin Art, Flash, Savage, Rebel Ink. A ton of lifestyle fetishes can be found here.

Taschen Books

Taschen books always has all kinds of crazy stuff:

http://www.taschen.com/pages/de/catalogue/sex/all.1.htm

Crossover Niches

There are a lot of mainstream niches and industries that tend to sway very close to the adult industry and may even include some fetish tendencies and potential as well.

I have found that in a lot of personal image, fashion, fitness or health oriented industries, there is the potential to meet a lot of adult entertainers and sex workers either current working as, or maybe who have left the adult biz in pursuit of other ventures. They may either have existing sites that need work, or are looking for an adult friendly designer to work on some of their new, non adult ventures.

Body building, workout, extreme fitness, tattoo, piercing, extreme sports and beauty care magazines will often times have a forum where you will have a good chance of either meeting some new clients or meeting people who may be interested in getting into adult and might be interested in your services.

Sometimes these forums will even have a special adult themed thread where you can discuss things openly.

Dating sites are also a great place to network with adult biz types. A lot of escorts and phone sex workers get involved in dating sites in order to lure new customers, so making your services know there can open a lot of doors as well.

Hot Tip:

I use a free note taking software called Evernote to keep track of all of my research. I keep a folder just for fetishes where I document all of my discoveries, screenshots, blog posts, photos, videos, etc. It features a handy web clipper extension for your browser, so whenever you discover something interesting, just highlight it and click the icon and it will make a note of it.

Evernote is a free cloud based service, so it stores all your data so you can access it in multiple places, on your machine, on the web or via iPhone/iPad. It has been an invaluable tool and a running journal of pretty much every idea I have.

http://evernote.com/

To summarize what you learned in this chapter:

1. There are riches in niches
2. A niche in adult is just another word for Fetish
3. People are into weird shit and there is fetish potential in everything
4. Fetish based communities offer the most potential for finding new clients and product ideas.
5. In order to find these, you need to dig deep, go spelunking and do your research.

Tip: Be sure to check out the "Big List of Fetishes" section at the end of this book for more ideas.

Chapter 9

The Portfolio

At this point, you should have enough of an overview of the industry, have settled on a few niche ideas and maybe even have spotted a few potential clients, so now is the time to start building up your adult design portfolio, so you can get them.

Despite what many people think, an effective portfolio doesn't need to be a super complicated undertaking.

From my experience, most potential clients who are considering hiring you, (and more importantly the one's that you should want to accept work from) are interested in the following key things:

- The quality of your work – Your design skills
- How quickly you work
- How reliable, professional and consistent you are
- How discreet and trustworthy you are
- Your level of knowledge about their niche/fetish
- Your Rates

What to include:

In my opinion, a solid, effective adult portfolio **should** include the following:

1. A simple, memorable brand

2. A clear USP (unique selling proposition) and a definition of what you do and what kind of services you provide. Ideally build around a keyword.
3. A good assortment of basic easy to browse design work examples
4. A mailing list sign up
5. Easy to find contact info (Email & social media connect links)
6. A very specific set of terms and services.
7. 2257 info in the footer.
8. Lot's of niche based keyworded text for SEO

Use Wordpress

This book isn't a tutorial or dissertation on Wordpress and as a designer, I would hope that you have a solid understanding of it, however if you don't for some reason, I highly suggest you spend a decent amount of time getting familiar with it and using it.

I started off when everyone still hand coded their websites and it was a real pain in the ass. I used to spend a lot of time on my portfolio design, but with the invention of blogging and content management systems such as Wordpress, I don't have to do that anymore.

If I can give you one piece of designer advice, focus more on sharpening your skills, marketing and client acquisition, instead of fucking around with your website all the time. Using a CMS (content management system) such as Wordpress will only make your life much more easy.

I now use Wordpress for my portfolio sites (actually I use it for pretty much everything these days) and it works perfectly for all of my needs.

I would suggest you do the same for the following reasons:

- It is easy and quick to manage
- It is dynamic and easily expandable
- Blogs get the best SEO

- Most of my clients base their online efforts around using Wordpress for good reason. If they don't already use it, they will eventually.

Not only will it make life much more simple for you, if you have wordpress skills, a whole universe of potential design, customization, installation and product ideas will open up for you.

Your clients WILL be asking for it, so it is a valuable skill worth mastering.

Check out: **http://www.wordpress.org**

Pick a Simple, Memorable, Luxury Brand

This sounds like a given but you will need a memorable brand and logo that represents your business.

Again, I am going to assume that since you are a designer, you should already have a decent understanding of the importance of strong branding as well as have the ability to come up with a good logo. I just want to emphasize that in this biz, you need one and most importantly, it needs to POP.

In the Adult Industry, you will be working with a lot of people who are incredibly image focused, materialistic and regardless of the niche, have a tendency to indulge in extravagance, luxury items and services.

Basically, they like bling.

Think of it this way. Most adult stars "do what they do" primarily because of the easy money and all of the things it can buy. Sure, some do it just because they like sex, but for the most part, it's the money,

They tend to spend a LOT of money on personal image, i.e. things and services that make them look good and feel good. Clothing, makeup, nice cars, luxury homes, hair dressers, manicures, cosmetic surgery, etc. They also will go out of their way to pay for services that provide high quality service and more importantly they can trust.

They won't think twice to blow $200 -$2000 or more on designer clothes or to get their "hair did" at a luxury salon with all the extras. **As a designer with this kind of clientele, you are also in the same line of business of making them look good** and this kind of service is expected from you.

As a result, you should position yourself immediately to BE one of these types of services and more importantly, so you can charge like one. Start off by establishing your business as luxury brand immediately, and save yourself the trouble of having to change it later. Be a chameleon. Bling is good!

Surprisingly, most designers fail miserably at this. You will have the advantage here, so take it.

Trust me, just do it. You'll thank me later.

My Brand

My brand is Devilish Media and my logo is a red flame with a circle around it. I used it on everything, from websites, to business cards, and most importantly, in social media profile pics.

It used to be the logo for my design business, but has evolved to represent my company as a whole.

Keep in mind that for the most part, you will be doing a majority of your customer acquisition via forums and social networks. If at all possible, try to come up with a logo that is easily recognizable in a small square user pic. Your user pic can be one of your strongest forms of advertising.

Define A Clear USP

In addition to your brand, you should include a USP, which stands for your Unique Selling Proposition. This is basically a simple statement about what your business is all about and ideally why it is different and worth hiring.

All good businesses have one, as it helps to tell the customer immediately what you do and why your business is special.

My USP started off as, "Affordable, Cutting Edge Adult Design Solutions."

I quickly learned that the "affordable" part was getting me a lot of clients, but was pretty much shooting me in the foot for the expectation of me making decent money, so eventually I settled on, simply:

"Adult Design Solutions"

This has worked for me just fine.

When deciding on your USP, try to think of all the companies and brands that you love or have a strong connection to and consider what their USP is.

Use an SEO Friendly USP

Here's a tip: When thinking of a USP, do some SEO keyword research and try to uncover what key phrases are being searched for by people looking to hire someone like you.

I'll give you a hint: a big one is "adult design" and it has helped me keep a pretty high ranking in the search engines.

Another example: If you have a lot of anime, hentai or tentacle sex designs in your portfolio then it would be to your advantage to make sure that somewhere on your site there is coded text that says something like: "adult design specializing in anime, hentai and tentacle sex websites."

Market Samurai

For keyword research I use a piece of software called Market Samurai. It has been an invaluable tool for not only getting my websites ranked better in the search engines, but also for doing niche and fetish research.

http://www.marketsamurai.com

Add Design Examples

The best part about adult design is that it is very predictable. As I mentioned before, regardless of the niche, it's all usually just a lot of images of people and skin with bright colors and text over it.

Because of this, it is relatively easy to get a decent portfolio together and be in business with just a handful of content and some key design examples.

Of course, the more, the better, but as long as your design skills are up to speed, the following are all fairly quick and easy to crank out. If you focus on these first, it will get you up and running much faster than if you spend a lot of time working on large, detailed examples.

Necessary:

- 3 - 5 banners of various sizes.
- A couple blog header graphics
- A couple full page ads (graphics)
- A couple basic membership site layouts (homepage screenshots)
- A couple twitter background images (or whatever social media profile flavor of the month)

Nice to have:

- Customized wordpress templates, (even if it's just a screenshot and not really coded)
- Blog designs

- Print Ads
- Erotic Book Covers
- DVD Box covers
- Sex toy product packaging
- Some profile listing designs (Niteflirt listings, cam sites, whatever is popular at the time)

As you do these, keep very close track of the time it takes to complete them (both good designs, and so-so designs) so you can base your time/pricing later (discussed in Getting paid) chapter.

Where to Get Adult Content?

Since this is adult design after all, you are going to need to use some adult content in your design examples. Since you haven't taken on any clients yet, you probably don't have any actual adult content from them to use, so problem becomes:

Where do you get some? Well, you've gotta go buy some adult content then!

Photo sets run anywhere from $10 to $300 depending on the seller and the quality. Most sets have around 20 to 50 images, with usually only 5 or 10 are really useful from a design standpoint.

To get started, I invested in about $200 worth of cheap content, which I just cropped and chopped, re-colored, reversed and reused for all kinds of basic example work.

A couple cheap $10 sets and a couple high quality sets should be enough for you to get started.

Keep these things in mind when buying Adult Content:

Buy content that works from a design perspective.

When you buy your content, try to keep in mind that, for most of your projects, you'll be taking the models in the images and squeezing them into tiny boxes of various sizes. This makes perspective, very important, so pay close attention to getting an assortment of images with poses that can fit both in a horizontal and in a vertical design space.

For example, a whole set of content where the model is primarily standing, is useless for horizontal banners and headers, which you may be creating a lot of. In fact, I would say from my experience, that most of my projects tend to require horizontal poses. Sure it works for skyscraper ads, but for the most part, I do horizontal.

When you start working with clients, also keep this in mind when discussing what content to use. It will save you a lot of time.

Make sure the content is legal and legit.

As I mentioned in the Legal section, I recommend NEVER featuring any actual nudity in your portfolio, so as long as you stick to this rule, getting sexy content isn't as hard as you might think.

Your portfolio still needs to be sexy, so I suggest only buying semi nude and softcore photo sets, instead of hardcore, then if there is any questionable nudity in it when the design is done, cover up the naughty bits with stars

Below is a list of cheap adult content providers, however you can also find a lot of decent softcore and basic sexy model photos (lingerie, bikini, semi nude) on stock photo sites, such as http://www.istockphoto.com

If you decide to buy actual adult related content however, make sure it comes with all the 2257 age verification information on the models. Each photo set you buy will usually include a photo of the model's ID, or them holding their ID, as well as a copy of the model contract they signed verifying their age.

If it doesn't come with this info, I highly suggest NOT buying it, because it is a sure sign that the content provider is NOT legit and the legal ramifications for YOU can be severe.

Content Provider Links:

A directory of content providers:

http://www.xbiz.com/directory/id=23&pid=3

A few reputable ones to check out:

http://www.bargainbasementcontent.com/

http://www.adultczechcontent.com/

http://market.adultcentro.com

The Mailing List

As I discussed in the strategy chapter, you should definitely use a mailing list with an auto responder, and the sign up form should be prominently displayed on your portfolio. If you use Wordpress, this is easy to add in the sidebar with a widget.

The incentive for joining your mailing list should ideally be something of value to the customer, so start off with a promotion offering a % off discount on services for anyone who joins the mailing list.

Mailing List Service Providers

In order to offer free items and opt in list subscribing, you will need to use some mailing list software that features an opt in and an autoresponder.

This means the customer has to first enter their email, then the system will send them an email that includes a confirmation link that they need to click on to activate their subscription. Once they activate, the system sends them another email that either contains the link where they claim their free stuff or a link to a page where their free stuff is located.

Which Mailing List software should you use?

There are a lot of mailing list providers, (Aweber and MailChimp are the biggies for internet marketing) however I have yet to find one that is cool with adult related promotions.

You can try to get away with using them, but usually if they catch you posting super adult related stuff, or even suspect it is mildly adult related, they can shut down your account.

You'll not only lose your fee that you pay them (these services can be expensive) but you'll lose your customer list, and you'll have to start all over again. Legally, you cant just migrate customers from on list to the other, so if your account does get shut down, you technically have to start all over again.

For this reason I suggest using your own software, so nobody can police what you can and cant say or do.

The Tribulant Newsletter Plugin

As I mentioned, I use Wordpress for all of my websites and I use a Newsletter plugin called Tribulant Newsletter. It allows you to keep your subscribers in your own database on your blog. The best part is that it is a plugin that you purchase, so there is no subscription or anyone policing what you write in your emails.

http://tribulant.com

Side Note: Running your mailing list off of Wordpress backend is probably not the most secure solution, however Tribulant, as of yet has been the most stable and inexpensive solution.

If you know of any other mailing list software options by the way, by all means use them (and send me an email letting me know!) Tribulant, however, so far has done the trick.

Protect your customer base by all means possible. It is your golden ticket to constant income, whenever you want it.

Terms & Services

Your TOS (Terms of Service) is your first line of defense when a potentially shitty customer comes creeping in like a vampire trying to suck you dry. (I say that lovingly...)

Usually, if you have cool clients, none of this will be necessary, but if you don't lay down the law upfront, when the time comes for someone to try to mess with you, you'll have nothing to point to and say, "...well, as it states clearly in my TOS...I don't do that shit..."

I'll have to be perfectly honest and state that I don't know what the legal limitations or obligations are regarding any of this, so this is not legal advice. I include a TOS usually just as a way to scare the shit out of anyone dumb enough to try to scam me. There are plenty of TOS generator programs out there that do a much better job with the legal stuff, but I create my own just so it covers all of my personal requirements.

Here are my exact TOS that I used on my site. If I even have the slightest hint of suspicion that a client is going to be "difficult", I will insist that they read my entire TOS before I agree to do any work for them:

A Sample of My Terms and Services:

- New clients will be required to pay 100% of the total balance in advance before work can commence, and may be required to sign a provided design agreement specifying the terms and scope of the project.

- We accept checks, money orders, and credit card payments, however, there will be a processing fee added to all payments made via credit card.

- Clients must provide all content, or we can refer them to some quality content providers. All provided content MUST be fully licensed by the Client and MUST have the proper certification proving that all models featured in the content are of legal age. Verification of this proof must be made available upon request.

- Clients must be at least 18 years of age or older, or of legal majority in their jurisdiction, to enter the site, request or order services from (your design company.

- Under no circumstances will (your design company) be liable/responsible for any damages or misuse resulting from the client's use of the designs, design services, or any content utilized in the design which was purchased from a third party. After the contract is finished, we have delivered the design and the client has made their final payment, we then have no legal connection. The client is responsible for their own actions.

- Under no circumstances will (your design company) be liable/responsible for any misuse, damages or service related issues regarding it's designs, products or services that were redistributed and purchased from someone other than (your design company).

- (your design company) does not provide free additional composite layouts. If the client requests additional layouts to choose from, we will be more than happy to provide as many as the client requests, but the client will still be charged at our standard hourly design rate.

- (your design company) reserves the right to use any products made by us in our portfolio unless a prior confidentiality agreement is in place with the client.

- If requested, we will provide design source material such as PSD and Flash files, however they must be requested in advance of the project and there will be an additional charge for such resources.

Please note that these points are just part of my personal TOS which is used in addition to the more official Terms of Service and Privacy Policy statements that all websites need to have.

There are several programs and services online that offer free TOS and Privacy Policy generators, so I suggest you research them and use them. They are for your own protection and you can never have enough of this stuff to help cover your ass. Having a lawyer help you write one also helps.

Social Media Accounts and Profiles

It is important to use social media as an extension of your portfolio and as a way to reach potential clients. As I mentioned before, it is the first touch point in the outer ring of your marketing funnel.

Even if you aren't ready to open up your business to customers yet, set your social accounts up ASAP. I suggest at a minimum, go to Twitter, Google + and Facebook and set up accounts and profiles for all of them. Twitter, being the most important.

Even if you just add your userpic and your portfolio URL, do this immediately. Ideally you should fill out your entire profile, with a solid description of your services. The more info, the better.

Don't List Prices

I'll get more into pricing later, so wait and read the next chapter before adding your rates to your portfolio.

For now however, as a personal piece of advice, if you feel like adding a few special offers in your sidebar, that's cool, but I personally don't list prices anymore. I always request that potential clients contact me for an estimate and let me know exactly what they need before quoting them a price.

1. This insures other designers and clients aren't doing any comparative shopping.

2. This helps to get an exact idea of everything they want.
3. By the tone of the email, you get an advanced feel for either how cool they are, or how much of an asshole they could potentially be.
4. This immediately sets the tone of the client relationship because people who request that you contact them for an estimate typically are the ones planning on charging more. This saves times, makes a statement and filters out the bargain hunters.

This will also insure that anyone who is really interested in your services will make the first move and send you an email. This part is half the battle, because if someone goes through all the work of writing an email inquiry, you can immediately assume that they are prequalified and ready to lay down some cash.

To summarize what you learned in this chapter:

1. Start a Wordpress portfolio with a small selection of key pieces
2. Pick a simple, memorable luxury brand name
3. Define a simple SEO friendly USP
4. Triple your rates out of the gate.
5. Buy sample content that works from a design perspective
6. Keep your content legal
7. Include a mailing list
8. Add a detailed TOS
9. Create your social accounts and get to know Twitter.
10. Don't post your rates upfront. Make them contact you for an estimate.

Chapter 10

Pricing and Billing

"When I was young, I thought that money was the most important thing in life. Now that I am old, I KNOW that it is."
– Oscar Wilde

Getting Paid Rule #1 - NEVER Work for Free

In regards to getting paid, let's get one thing perfectly clear.

NEVER work for free.

You don't do pro bono work, you don't do free comps, you don't EVER work for free. The second you start offering free work will be the second you might as well dump your career down the toilet. Seriously. You can do it later when you're old and have a solid retirement fund saved up, but not now.

As in all industries, Adult more so then ever, people will bang on you for spec work until the end of time.

They will demand it. They will plead and bitch and moan and whine when you don't. They will try to invalidate and patronize you about it. They will offer you cocaine and sex in return for it. They will call you every name in the book and threaten to slander you all over the industry if you don't comply, but YOU WILL NOT DO IT.

I don't care if Hugh Hefner himself calls you up and asks for it, you DO NOT work for free.

Understood? Good.

So what do you do when this topic comes up?

Getting Paid Rule #2 - Become a Master of the Art of Fuck You

Get into the habit of practicing the art of Fuck You.

On occasion, I accept consulting roles. I am very particular who I accept and I don't take just anyone. I charge a very high rate for my services because I am worth it.

Always remember, you are a professional. You offer a sought after, valuable creative skill that not everyone can do. You have a portfolio full of satisfied clients who make much more money as a result of your work, then before they hired you.

Not to brag here, but let's put this into perspective.

I am very good at what I do. I can turn someone into a millionaire as a result of my services. I know adult design, mainstream design, internet marketing, sales, user experience, information architecture and the psychology behind what makes it all successful. I work for myself, I am self taught, I have never gone to college, and my clients include famous rock stars, actors, porn stars, authors, politicians and Fortune 500 Companies.

These people rely on me to help make them more money and the smart ones are willing to pay me for that opportunity. My business is for ninjas only. Ninja services for ninja customers. No hackers allowed.

I want my clients to succeed. I want them to look like the most irresistible sex goddess that their customers have ever seen and as a result, I want them to make truckloads of money. To do this it takes skill, time attention to detail, knowledge and experience.

One parasitic variable in the form of a potential difficult client can cost you millions in time and resources. Avoid them like the plague. You are a professional. You are the best designer in the business and you are worth every dollar you charge. If you don't believe it and act like it, someone else sure will.

If a potential client wants free work, or causes you any level of undeserved complaint whatsoever, Fuck You!

Many of my clients are professional dominatrixes. Most of them are super cool clients. I respect them and they respect me. On rare occasions however, some amateur will try to treat me like one of their customers and try to "dom" me. This is followed by a quick and courteous "fuck off".

If they have any brains at all, they will see the error of their ways and apologize. Sure, I can understand that sometimes they just get too involved in their personas and forget who you are, so sometimes they just need a reality check.

You will earn respect quickly for this. Yes, it's all about customer service, but it is also about having the balls to say "Fuck no and Fuck You!"

So now that we have that out of the way, how exactly do you get paid?

Getting Paid Rule #3 - Get the Money Upfront

NEVER Ever EVER take a project without getting a deposit first before you do the work. I personally demand 100% of the fee upfront.

This may seem unreasonable, but I look at it this way: I have a public portfolio of satisfied clients and testimonials. I make a point of making myself visible to the world and upholding my reputation. My work is good and I am worth the money I charge.

Most of my clients however, have nothing but an obscure email as a point of contact.

So, when the question comes up as to how trustworthy you are, who is more suspect here?

If a client can't afford to pay you upfront, then they certainly cant afford to pay you in installments. Better to just say no then negotiate fees you may never see. The best thing you can do is get it all up front.

Forget Contracts

While negotiating design contracts for mainstream projects is a normal way of doing things, in adult, I have found it to be a waste of time. I've tried it and most of them shrink back in fear like vampires to garlic.

My clients live in a world of high risk and constant fear of legal action, so asking them to sign a legally binding contract, especially if it includes their real name is a waste of time.

Your best option, instead of contracts, is to get the money up front. This is simple, safe and works out best for you. It is much less time consuming too. Spending time drawing up contract for a $500 job is pointless. Forget about it.

Getting Paid Rule #4 - Be Officially Nondescript on Paper

Accepting credit card payments is one of the most challenging aspects for any company in the adult biz. It is literally something that makes and breaks adult businesses from one day to the next, and along with age verification and obscenity laws, one of the banes of our existence.

More and more, due to various liability reasons, billing companies are cracking down on adult related billing activities and making it harder and harder to get paid. Often times it's not completely unheard of that a billing company will change their policies and shut down an account seemingly overnight, with no warning, sometimes with no explanation.

Unfortunately, unless you want to sit around and wait for old school checks to show up via snail mail, running an online business in a global economy relies on being able to take credit cards. It is unavoidable.

Because of this, I suggest you do the following:

Since you are most likely just starting out in the biz and don't have a bazillion dollars to set up an expensive, high risk merchant account, here is a suggestion.

Pick a nondescript business name.

When setting up your business, don't choose an adult themed business name on paper. Don't start off by calling yourself something like Joe's Adult Porn Design. Instead, lay low. Pick a business name that is very mainstream and nondescript.

"Dynamic Creative Services", or "Super Duper Media Co". or something like that. You can call yourself whatever you want on your website, your domain name or anything customer facing, but on paper, when you bill, or at least when you sign up for any kind of financial related services, keep it clean and nondescript.

When I bill clients, in the description of services, I only state "Design fees". That's it. Don't make the mistake of writing in the notes, "Design fee for anal fisting and bondage banners"

If you are a design business, there is nothing wrong with billing someone for "design services" and when it comes to online billing processors, there is no reason to have to be more descriptive.

Make it a point as well, to educate your customers about online billing protocol as well. Usually the pro clients will already know this, but if you deal with newbie clients, be sure to educate them about not only keeping the descriptive text and wording clean, but also to use email addresses that are clean too.

I also suggest that you set up your billing account with a non adult email address and make sure your clients do the same.

If mistresswhoreslutfuck@bondageexplosion.com is your client, make sure they use their janedoe@whatev.com email instead.

This simple practice will mean the difference between the ability to get paid and losing your billing account forever, for both you and your clients. Don't slip up. Be smart about this.

Billing Services

So what billing services should you use? I debated discussing this, however at the risk of leaving out some vital info in a resource such as this book, I feel it would be more logical to just say that adult friendly online billing services come and go like the wind these days.

If at all possible, you should seriously consider setting up a high risk billing account with one of the handful of processors that handle a majority of the adult business accounts. Having an account like this will cost you a little money, but in the long run, it will pay for itself, if only for the security and stability.

When deciding on what billing processor to use, make it a regular point to browse the adult webmaster forums and ask for advice on who to use and who is available currently.

I find that Xbiz.net has some of the most professional members and many of them own or work for online billing processors, so it would be to your best advantage to get to know them personally, and see how they can take care of your billing needs.

Getting Paid Rule #5 - You Don't Charge Enough

Regarding rates, I really can't tell you what to charge. It is up to you to determine how much time it takes to do something, so figure that out and charge accordingly.

Whatever it is that you charge however, I know from experience that it's not enough. The best advice I can offer you is that once you have that magic number figured out. Triple it. Seriously.

You're worth it and your clients need to know that up front. Raising your rates later in the future only causes problems and if you set the bar high up front, there is nowhere to go but up.

How to Blow Away the Competition

Here's a super secret tactic for blowing away the competition. When deciding how to charge, the first thing I did was go commando and spy on the competitors. Chances are, if they offer average design quality, they are most likely either mid priced or have been drinking the "adult industry is on the decline" Kool-Aid and are lowballing their rates in order to keep the business coming in.

As crazy as this sounds, when breaking into the biz, the best thing you can do is drop in like a bomb by immediately doubling or even tripling what anyone else charges. This might go against conventional thinking, but this will do two psychological things:

1. Your prospective clients who, up until now, have been hiring the competition, will immediately start to question the quality of the, now, cheaper services they have been receiving. Immediately the other designers will start to look cheap.

Remember what I talked about in the Strategy section? Porn starts don't like cheap. They want the best. They want the luxury goods and suddenly their bad ass expensive designer looks ghetto. Uh oh…

2. The competition will either call you stupid or start to question the quality of their work as well. "What makes this guy so much of a bad ass that they can charge like that? They will NEVER be able to make that kind of money for a banner or a Wordpress install… what a sucker… what's he got that I don't? Hmmm… ???"

Because of this thinking, they will either stay firm and try to validate their prices, launch some ridiculous sale or else they will freak out and triple their prices as well. Most likely this will only serve as confusion to their customers and make them angry and confused, whereby making you look more in control and legit.

I have to admit this method works really well. I have done it in 3 different industries and I get the same results every time. It might take a little time to have an effect, but it's like a boiling kettle on the stove. Eventually it blows over and you will rake in the benefits in a slow steady flow of new and well paying customers.

To summarize what you learned in this chapter:

1. Never EVER work for free
2. Learn the art of Foo Kyoo
3. Get the money upfront
4. Never demand contracts
5. Stay officially nondescript on paper
6. You don't charge enough
7. Triple your rates out of the gate and explode the competition.

Chapter 11

Open for Business!

At this point, you should have your portfolio set up and your brain should be so crammed full of new and useful information about the adult industry that you should be ready to jump in and get some clients.

How do you get Clients?

I'll let you in on a little secret. The basic formula for getting clients in the adult biz is the same for any biz these days in the new social media focused business world, which is:

- Establish Presence
- Get Social
- Establish Authority
- Create a free offer & capture leads on your mailing list
- Use your mailing list to market your services or anything else you think they might be interest in that you could profit from.
- Repeat

Establish Presence

One of the most effective ways to find new clients, is to establish a social presence by participating and being active on the adult forums and social networks.

About 75% of my business comes from networking on forums and continues to be the most reliable way to establish your credibility in the adult community and maintain a steady flow of clients.

Remember, your focus here is B2B and your clients are in the Adult Biz. Because of this, stick with adult related resources for promoting your services.

Here's how you get your first adult design job:

1. If you haven't already done so, make sure you complete your portfolio as discussed in the portfolio chapter.

2. Go to **http://www.xbiz.net** & sign up. Make sure your profile is filled out. Don't forget to add a profile pic and the link to your portfolio and any other social media links) Note: You'll need a portfolio link in order to sign up.

3. Write a message introducing yourself, and describe what you do.

Here is an example message that works perfectly:

"Hi everyone! I am new to the forum and just wanted to introduce myself. My name is (your name) and I am a designer and I have an adult design business called (your design business).

I specialize in (list the kind of design that you specialize in #1, 2, 3...)

I am currently open for new projects and looking forward to meeting everyone, networking and building some new business relationships.

*You can check out my portfolio at www.yourportfolio.com
If you like what you see, my email is on my contact page and I would love to hear from you.*

Thanks for your time and I look forward to getting to know you all"

That's it

If you do this and you have a solid portfolio based on what was discussed, I am about 90% positive, that within a couple days (if not hours) someone will be in contact with you for your first project. Having red this book completely, you should be confident enough to take the job and do some good work.

While you are waiting for some responses, check out all the other adult industry forums listed in the resource section of this book. These forums tend to come and go quite often, so also Google "adult webmaster forums" for anything new. Then go to all of these sites and do the same thing.

If you have already chosen to cater to some type of niche, then it is even more important to find some industry related forums for that niche as well.

Before posting this message on the forums, make sure that you check the forum rules and make sure you post in the proper thread. Usually there is a "Say Hello" or an "announce yourself" kind of thread where the moderator allows you to do this.

HUGE TIP - follow the moderators rules and stay friendly with them. Better yet, write the mod first and ask where the best place to announce yourself on the forum would be. Usually they will be happy to tell you and often times will give you a nice personal introduction to the rest of the forum.

Be Professional

As in any business, credibility is a must. Adult is no different. People want to know that when they hire you, they can trust you. Often times as a designer you are privy to lots of personal information, real names, addresses, billing info, their FTP or server info, access to their entire content library and of course plenty of naked pictures of either them or their wives, girlfriends, boyfriends, husbands, etc.

Flaming Happens

Due to the nature of the biz, there can be a LOT of douchebags that you will come into contact with in adult. The biz is also very good at policing itself, so regardless of the "in your face" attitude of the industry, nobody who has any real brains and makes any real money likes to have drama, and for the most part, people like to stay low key.

There can also be a LOT of assholes on adult message boards, so be forewarned. These are primarily the ones who are busy running their mouths off instead of making money anyway, so as a rule of thumb, I don't engage with anyone who is too obnoxious and avoid flame wars.

Regardless, it is pretty unavoidable that you will post a message and not get "some" level of shit from someone, so my best advice is to keep cool and stay as professional as possible.

Being nice goes a LONG way and if people sense that you are trying to be professional and non confrontational, it is also a good sign that you would be a decent person to work with.

Social Media

The next step is to start establishing your social media presence. If you completed all the steps in the Portfolio chapter, you should already have some social profiles set up. The next step is to "pepper" these profiles with updates and content so you can establish that you have been active and look legit.

If you use a Wordpress blog for a portfolio, it is super easy to just make a post whenever you update your portfoilio. Simple stuff like that helps to fill up your social timelines until you have more relevant stuff to post about.

Social media is the best way to broadcast messages that result in people going to your portfolio and opting in to your mailing list, so your main posting strategy beyond communication should include lots of regular calls to action to feed the funnel.

The Best Social Networks for Adult

At the time of this writing, the best social networks for adult are as follows:

Xbiz.net – http://www.xbiz.net

Xbiz.net is one of the leading adult industry social networks. It is a great place to get started, meet industry related people and businesses and I suggest starting there.

Twitter - http://www.twitter.com

Twitter.com tends to be pretty lenient on adult activity, so a majority of my clients use it as their primary social network. Setting up a Twitter account should be a must have, and getting familiar with it, if you haven't already should be at the top of your list.

Make sure your profile description includes a link to your portfolio and your description should include your keywords, such as Adult Design. Make it a daily point of following adult industry related people and businesses, and you will quickly get follow backs and build your following.

The way I approach Twitter is to follow as many people as I can, who fit the bill as my typical customer. Following people usually will get a decent percentage of follow backs and as a result, you will also get followers filtering down from their followers. Most adult businesses and entertainers will follow back other adult businesses just because of this fact.

Take a look at my Twitter followers list:
https://twitter.com/devilishmedia

There are nearly 1000 people on that list and a majority of them are adult entertainers, mostly PSOs. If you want customers, find another adult biz with a list of the same kinds of potential customers and follow them all.

You can start with my list. It's ok, we're all players here. I wont resent you for it.

Take it slow though. Don't follow like 1000 people in a day or Twitter might get cranky with you. Try 50 or so a week and see what happens.

Google + - https://plus.google.com/

Because of the social circles, Google + offers a lot of potential for adult and there seems to be a pretty decent group of adult businesses experimenting with the new service. G+ is another great place for B2B networking, so I suggest you go there, establish a page and get involved. Google is not going anywhere anytime soon, and it has a lot of potential for improving your SEO, so use it.

Linkedin – http://www.linkedin.com

Linkedin.com used to be just for mainstream business networking, however due to the fact that there are private groups as well as being the central networking location for affluent customers, a lot of my clients are starting to show up and experiment with promoting themselves on LinkedIn. There are also a lot of adult industry related groups on there, so a simple search will turn some up. At the time of this writing it is still a pretty untapped resource and has a lot of upward potential to establish yourself there. Jump in now!

Some notable Adult Business groups on Linkedin at the time of this writing are:

The Adult Industry Trade Association

http://www.linkedin.com/groups?gid=3817081

Adult Industry Professionals

http://www.linkedin.com/groups?gid=956427

Adult Industry Networking

http://www.linkedin.com/groups?gid=4451002

Facebook – http://www.facebook.com
(do I really need to post a link??)

There is a lot of talk about Facebook.com for business these days, but for Adult, I find it to be not the best platform. By all means take advantage of it as a traffic source, however keep in mind that most people use Facebook for more personal types of networking, such as family & friends.

The likelihood that someone will "Like" and engage with an adult related Facebook page is low because this action is visible to their friends as well. The majority of my clients also use fictional personas (which Facebook frowns upon) so for the most part, this is not your audience. (Or at least not that they want to admit too with their friends watching)

Facebook also takes a pretty strict stance against adult related activity, so if you do use Facebook, keep it clean, professional and informative, but don't post any nudity, or you will get banned. It is definitely worth experimenting with because as we all know, there are like a gazillion people on there now, but proceed with caution.

Xpeeps – http://www.xpeeps.com

XPeeps is a customer facing social network for people who like porn. It is kind of an dating site and kind of a dumping ground for escorts, porn stars and cam girls to post their profiles. It has been around for a while and has seen a lot of changes. Definitely worth making a profile there because it is full of potential clients.

Meetme – http://www.meetme.com

Meetme (formerly MyYearbook) is a pretty large social network that is a little bit like facebook and a little bit like a dating site. It has a lot of cool features, games, virtual economy, etc. that make it a very stick place to network and it also has a lot of adult entertainers trolling around, especially cam girls who will try to lure you into a pay chat. I have met quite a few clients here, so it is definitely another good place to check out on a very casual level.

Pinterest – http://www.pinterest.com

Pinterest is a relatively new social network where people can post photos and videos. It has primarily a female demographic, however it is catching on with mainstream business and is also popular with the erotica crowd. You have to be subtle with Pinterest, however your posts can get you a TON of traffic so it is worth experimenting with, at least for posting related interests, soft core portfolio screens, etc.

Add Your Social Icons to Your Portfolio

Be sure not to forget to add your social icons on your portfolio page to make your customers aware that you have social media accounts.

Whenever I join a new social network, I also make a point of posting and sending an email informing my clients of it's benefits and asking them to join me there.

Read Mashable

http://www.mashable.com

Mashable is probably the most reliable source for all up to date social media related news. I make it a point to read Mashable daily and whenever they post about some new and upcoming social network, I jump on it and either sign up or join the waiting list.

Getting a head start on all new social networks will insure you are on the cutting edge as well as ahead of the curve for any potential traffic or clients should the network take off.

Establish Authority - Become a Moderator Yourself

Once you start getting a reputation as a knowledgeable designer and a respected member of the adult community, you might want to consider becoming a moderator on one of these forums.

I was a design forum moderator on a couple different sites and the connections I made from doing this were priceless. Being a mod boosts your credibility 1000% and just from the word of mouth reputation alone, new clients will be flying in by the truckload.

Hot Tip!

As I've mentioned, a lot of my clients are dominatrixes. I was lucky in that I already had a few clients who liked my work and introduced me in to those circles, so word of mouth was all I needed to build a solid reputation and grow a large client list.

If you're just starting out however, you might not have this type of reputation built up yet, so you may need to do a little cold calling at first.

So, where do you find a bunch of Dominatrixes in need of design who you can call up? Check this out.

Dominant Directory International Magazine

I was in the magazine rack at the train station and stumbled across this gem of a resource. It is the **World Edition of the Dominant Directory International**, which is basically a huge quarterly directory of pro Dominatrixes from all around the world, including photos, phone numbers, emails and domain names.

http://www.ddimag.com/

If you can pick up a recent copy, you will be in possession of a goldmine of client potential. It is mostly customer facing contact info, but I would be willing to bet you could get a couple new clients lined up in no time with the contact info that is in there.

Some other resources are: http://www.xdpublications.co.uk/

Home of Pro Domme Magazine and Little Black book. Some other great Domme resources.

Feed and Nurture Your Lists:

If you followed my advice in the strategy and portfolio sections, you should have a mailing list sign up already set up on your portfolio page and based on the actions in this chapter, your lists should be starting to grow in members.

I can't stress how important it is to get people to follow you via social media and then get people to join your list. This is the number one tool you have for successfully communicating with your clients, announcing your availability, special offers, services and growing a following.

Even if every other social network, forum or advertising platform should fail or go out of business, you will always have your mailing list as a fall back for engaging with your clients.

Grow and nurture your list and your business will grow with it.

To summarize what you learned in this chapter:

1. Establish Presence
2. Get Social
3. Establish Authority
4. Create a free offer & Capture Leads on your mailing list
5. Use your mailing list to market your services or anything else you think they might be interest in that you could profit from.

Chapter 12

Marketing Tips & Tricks

The following are some tips and tricks I use to squeeze in some extra cash, clients or traffic.

Start Your Own Adult Sites

After you start to get a hang of how adult websites work and monetize, there is nothing stopping you from launching some of your own. You can either start your own member's sites or just make money promoting your clients sites as an affiliate and maybe you even get first crack at their content.

I've personally tried my hand at a few adult blogs and gallery sites promoting affiliate links and content. As a result, I managed to make a pretty decent passive income from them and have since sold these websites off for a decent profit.

My most favorite of all the adult sites I have owned was a blog called Porn is Boring, where I basically just talked shit about whatever adult site I could dig up and how stupid people were for looking at it and paying for it. Surprisingly, it ended up being my highest converting website. Porn is Boring? Who would have thunk it?

Free Ebooks

A great way to build traffic and grow your subscriber list is to write some informational ebooks, reports and white papers and give them away for free. It's not necessary to write a lengthy book however, so don't let that intimidate you. They can easily be just a few pages of specific information that solves a problem for your customer, such as where to get the best web hosting, why they should use Wordpress, how to write copy for SEO, maybe even, how to choose the right designer for their needs.

The goal of the ebook is to:

1. Offer free advice so that you appear to be the authority on a particular subject so people will feel confident in wanting to hire you.

2. Include a decent call to action (or many) in the book that invites the reader to go to your website and sign up to your mailing list.

People love to share useful ebooks, especially when it is about a very unique and specialized interest, so you will be surprised how widely distributed your free material will get, and your traffic will grow like crazy. It takes a little time but this is a very effective long term strategy.

Offer Incentive for Promotion

For a while I was giving my best customers a special badge to feature on their blogs, which said "Official Devilish Girl" and featured a ribbon and a gold medal with my logo. The graphic then linked back to a page on my site that featured the work that I did for them and confirming they were part of the extra prestigious Devilish Girl Club.

Some customers didn't use it, but others loved to show off on their websites that they hire only the best, and as a result, I got a lot of traffic and new customers who all wanted to be part of my super special club.

Platinum Club

As my services became harder and harder to book, for my extra, extra special clients, I created an Invite Only Platinum Club Service. For a sizable, but reasonable monthly fee, this service basically held me in retainer so that the client would always have me readily available to book as a top priority whenever they needed design.

This was limited to only a small handful of clients so that it wouldn't get out of hand, however most of the time they would forget to use the service after they paid for it, so as a result, I made some pretty decent monthly cash for basically nothing.

Make Swag

On occasion I would offer some limited edition t-shirts, mugs and stickers with my logo on it for sale. Clients love that stuff, especially if you give it away as a free gift.

Get your super sexy clients to send you a photo of them wearing your t-shit and post it on your site. You'll look extra pimpin!

Provide World Class Customer Service

Before I wrap up this book, I would like to leave you with a few thoughts and some advice.

Unfortunately, everything you have learned in this book, up until now, has only been the first step. Once the customer acquisition phase is over and the client has trusted enough in you to give you their deposit, it is now game on.

Beyond this point, *it is up to you to provide world class customer service* in order to show to your clients and the rest of the industry that your services are worth every penny of what you charge and what you have claim to deliver.

The majority of this book has, for all intents and purposes, been about the seduction, the marketing, researching and attracting of new customers. Once this part is over however, it is then up to you to bust your ass and treat your customers like royalty.

Remember, you are the luxury boutique and you want your customers to walk out feeling like a million bucks. You want them drooling over the thought of all the money your work will make them. You want them bragging to all of their jealous friends about how amazing you are.

I can't hold your hand beyond this point, because customer service, like design is an art form that has to be learned by doing. I can tell you, however, that without a doubt, I have managed to base my entire business reputation not so much on on the quality of my design skills, which is a given, but more importantly on providing the best service possible. It has been my calling card and has proven to be very lucrative.

If you adopt this way of thinking, you will always have the competitive advantage, regardless of your skill level.

Some thoughts to leave you with:

- Be immaculate and precise in everything you do.
- Respond to EVERY email even if you know they are broke.
- THANK your customers. Every email I respond to starts with "Hi and thanks for contacting me,"
- Be respectful of their idiosyncrasies. There will be many.
- Never break a promise. Your word is golden and set in stone.
- Continuously learn and practice your skills. It will show in your work.
- Be discreet. This business is all about trust, so respect confidentiality.
- Never leave an inquiring client hanging. If they want to hire you and you say no, then always refer them to another designer. Your clients are coming to you for help. Always offer a solution and add value at every opportunity. It will be remembered.
- Be better than a mainstream business. The adult industry is always under fire for being deceitful and sleazy. Prove them 200% wrong.
- Your customer service skills are more important than your design skills. I'm sorry to say so, but it's true. A shitty design delivered with class, on time and as promised will be valued far and above an awesome design delivered poorly and with difficulty.
- Most Importantly: People are into a lot of weird and kinky shit, so get out there, dig it up and sell it to them!

Shocking Secrets of Adult Design

Summary

I hope that you found the info in this book useful and that by now your brain should be buzzing with all kinds of new ideas for new opportunities, new niches & new strategies to grow your business.

The most important thing you can do now is to TAKE ACTION immediately and apply what you have learned. So, put this book down now and get to work!

Don't forget to tell your friends how awesome it was though. ;)

I wish you the best of luck and I look forward to hearing all about your twisted tales of success in your newly found pornographic business ventures.

- Sean

Contact Me

If you have any questions or comments about the business and marketing of adult design or anything else in this book, feel free to contact me via the info below or leave a comment on the blog and I will try to respond as soon as possible.

Email: **devilishmedia@gmail.com**

Twitter: **http:twitter.com/devilishmedia**

More Cool, Devilish Stuff

For more cool marketing books and products just like this one, be sure to check out the Devilish Media website at:

http://www.devilishmedia.com

Resources

Adult Industry Conventions

The Adult Entertainment Expo
http://show.adultentertainmentexpo.com

The Internext Expo
http://www.internext-expo.com

Suggested reading list:

"The Four Hour Workweek" by Tim Ferris

"No BS Marketing to The Affluent" by Dan Kennedy

"Uncensored Sales Strategies" By Sidney Biddle Barrows

"Sex, Money, Kiss!" by Gene Simmons

"Pitch Anything" by Oren Klaff

"Start Your Own Information Marketing Business" by Entrepreneur Press

Sign up For AVN Online

http://www.xbiz.com/digital/

Adult Resources List

Cozy Frog
http://www.cozyfrog.com

Xbiz
http://www.xbiz.com

Xbiz.net
http://www.xbiz.net

GFY
http://www.gofuckyourself.com

AVN
http://business.avn.com

Netpond
http://www.netpond.com

Ynot
http://www.ynot.com

Ynot Europe
http://www.ynoteurope.com

Green guy and Jim
http://www.greenguyandjim.com

Adult Chamber
http://www.adultchamber.com

Adult Forums 247
http://www.adultforums247.com

Mainstream Internet Marketing Forums that Discuss Adult:

Digitalpoint
http://forums.digitalpoint.com/

The Warrior Forum
http://www.warriorforum.com/

Erotic Author Resources

Literotica
http://literotica.com

The Erotica Readers and Writers Association
http://erotica-readers.com

Content Providers

The Xbiz Content Provider Directory
http://www.xbiz.com/directory/id=23&pid=3

Bargain Basement Content
http://www.bargainbasementcontent.com/

Adult Czech Content
http://www.adultczechcontent.com/

Chemical Content
http://chemicalcontent.com/

Adult Centro
http://market.adultcentro.com

Scarlet Content
http://www.scarlettcontent.net/

Adult Content NL
http://www.adultcontent.nl/

About the Author

Sean Earley is a marketing consultant, designer, writer of unconventional business and marketing resources and pin-up artist extraordinaire. His primary focus is in helping to educate companies and small businesses on how to best leverage new technology, marketing, design and social media to reach their goals and increase their bottom line.

You can learn more about him on his website at:

www.seanearley.com

For more great marketing related products, check out:

www.devilishmedia.com

& Join the Mailing List!

Made in the USA
Las Vegas, NV
08 April 2021